in

Rhymes

A Collection of Grace Poems

Kathy H. Rasnake

Grace In Rhymes
A Collections of Poems by Kathy Rasnake

Grace In Rhymes
Copyright ©2020 by Kathy Rasnake

First Printing - 2020

ISBN   9798564405423 (KDP)

DEDICATION

This book is dedicated to my Father, my Mother and Jesus. Between them they gave me temporal life and eternal life. Without them, I would literally be nothing...

ACKNOWLEDGEMENTS

Besides the Lord Himself, there are a few people I'd like to acknowledge for their love, support and encouragement.

Brad Robertson, without your generous offer of help and the time that you invested putting this book together, *Grace In Rhymes* might never have happened! Thank you so much, my brother in Christ! I pray we both meet souls in heaven who were touched by these little rhymes.

Robin Fondurulia, Cindy Tham, and Ashley Silva, thank you for the encouragement and feedback you gave me as I wrote these grace rhymes and shared them on Facebook. Your love and fellowship has been a source of joy and comfort.

Daniel Lingerfelt, thank you for watching over me like a son and a brother in Christ.

Friends and family, thoughts of you often crossed my mind along with the rhymes. God bless you all for your love and inspiration.

KHR

FORWARD

When I first read one of Kathy's poems, I knew she had a unique gift, the gift of putting grace into poems. I first saw her poems on Facebook years ago and always enjoyed reading her next post about God's grace.

Over the years, I have watched Kathy post the most wonderful poems about God's grace. Her poems have impacted the lives of many people as they have come to experience God's grace in rhymes.

I am so excited to see Kathy's poems of grace compiled into a book...*Grace In Rhymes*.

I envision *Grace In Rhymes* sitting on living room tables in homes all over the world. I envision people casually picking up the book to read a few poems, not realizing they are about to read poems that are so powerful their lives will change forever as they encounter God's grace with every rhyme.

On behalf of all your Facebook friends, I want to thank you Kathy for sharing your gift of writing grace poems that have impacted our lives, and now, through *Grace In Rhymes*, will impact the lives of people all over the world!

Brad Robertson
Author of *The Story of Grace*

A DREAM WITHIN

A long time ago,
I had a dream within my heart,
That I could write a book,
The grace of God to impart.

Life washed me up
On some rough and rocky shores.
The dream was abandoned,
And I thought of it no more.

But God was the Gardener
Who had planted the dream in my heart,
And the will and desire
Were His from the start.

So, I pray the ones who read
These little rhymes of mine
Will know they were grown
From seeds that God watered over time.

PORTRAIT

Lord, make me a portrait
Of your love and grace.
When others look at me,
Let them see Your face.

Let the words I speak
Be like refreshing rain from above,
Golden fruit from my lips,
Showering thirsty souls with Your love.

Let my hands be diligent
To provide what others need,
Let them minister comfort,
To souls that in sorrow grieve.

1 John 4:17; Hebrews 13:15-16;
Proverbs 25:11; Galatians 6:9-10;
2 Thessalonians 3:13; Galatians 6:2; Galatians 2:20

GET A CLUE

It took me nearly thirty-seven years to get a clue,
About doctrines and truth, I thought that I knew.

I listened to the preachers who claimed they were right,
And swallowed what they fed me without even a fight.

They told me my sins I must daily confess,
Or God would not hear me and they would pile up in a big
brushy mess.

They said God would break off His fellowship with me,
Until I wept and repented on my bended knees;

But After I did that then God would be pleased,
And once again shine His favor on me.

With sin as my focus and their rules as my guide,
I was told my "sinful nature" could be nearly, but not quite set
aside.

They said I would always have two dogs fighting within, and the
one I fed most with discipline or license would eventually win.
So, now I was TWO people according to them.

Next, they told me that while on earth I could never be
completely sanctified, for there were steps involved before I
could be holy and then glorified.

They said, I had "positional righteousness" but that it was only
in God's eyes.

The implication was that in truth and practice I was still the
same old mess,

But if I worked hard at it I could come close to passing their holier than thou tests.

They fed me this leaven until I believed it was true,
And the WORST thing is that I passed this fakery on too!

I thank God for the people who gently dropped me some clues,
And for the Holy Spirit Who caused me to see that I'd been fed corrupt food.

Now, I believe what the Word of God says is literally true!
I'm a new creation through and through!

My identity in Christ is absolutely true.
I'm complete in Him and Holy too!

I'm as "right as rain" in my born-again heart,
For Jesus Christ resides there, the new man, never to depart!

So, how could God turn away from His Own precious ones,
When Jesus died on a cross crying that the battle is won!?

The truth is, the moment I believed the gospel was true,
I died, was buried, and rose again too and the "old man" I'd been was replaced by the new!

I often wonder why I believed for so many years that false doctrine was true,
And why it took me so long to get a clue, when the Word of God plainly says believers are brand new!

THE SCRIPTURE:
Romans 6:3-7; Romans 6:17-18;
Romans 6:20-23; Ephesians 2:4-6;
2 Corinthians 5:17; Galatians 2:20;
Hebrews 10:1-17; Ephesians 2:1-3; Colossians 2:9-17

Mary

As a little girl in Nazareth,
How was she to know,
She would birth the One
Foretold many moons ago?

She was just a humble virgin
From a family once renown,
Espoused to a carpenter
From the same background.

Yet, in the course of ordinary life,
A miracle came upon her,
When Gabriel, the messenger,
Appeared to say she was chosen by her Maker,

To be the one long prophesied
To bear the Savior of her people,
The One to crush the serpent's head,
The Good Shepherd of the sheepfold.

To the angel's request,
She humbly acquiesced,
And in Bethlehem she gave birth,
There first holding Him to her breast.

She watched in wonder
As He grew in stature and in favor,
Treasuring in her heart
The words spoken by her Creator.

Yet, the shadow of the cross
Lay upon her inward part,

Because she had also been told
A sword would pierce her heart.

She loved and followed Him
From cradle to the cross.
How was she to know so many years ago
That Heaven's gain would be her loss?

Luke 1:26-31; Luke 1:38; Luke 2:19;
Luke 2:25-35; Luke 2:39-40;
Luke 8:19-20; John 19:25-27;
Genesis 3:15; Colossians 2:9-15

"IT IS FINISHED!"

These three words thrill my soul,

Because they mean I can rest in Christ minus worry and toil!

Born in Adam, we're all the spiritually walking dead,

But the moment we receive Him, we are born again instead!

This miracle called regeneration, brought about by grace through faith,

Places us in Christ, eternally kept and safe!

The gospel goes one step further than simply forgiveness for our sins.

The gospel also says that we died on the cross with Him,

And just as Jesus rose up from the grave in resurrection light,

We also rose up with Him as His espoused bride,

United in one spirit with His Holy Seed inside.

John 19:30; Ephesians 2:5-9;
Ephesians 2:1; 2 Corinthians 5:17;
John 10:27-30; Romans 6:4-8;
Galatians 2:20; Romans 7:4;
2 Corinthians 11:2; 1 John 3:9

NEW WINE

I drink from a cup
That contains Christ's blood.
He went to the winepress ratifying a New Covenant,
Written in His own precious blood.

Conceived before time began,
This New Covenant depends no way on me,
It was cut between the Father and the Son,
And will stand for all eternity!

All that it contains,
Means I'm as safe as I can be,
And by the power of an endless life,
I am assured eternal security!

Luke 5:37-39; Matthew 26:26-29;
John 6:47-63; Isaiah 63:1-3; Ephesians 1:3-7; Hebrews 4:3;
1 Peter 1:18-23; Hebrews 7:15-17;
Hebrews 7:19-28

RESTORED

In the beginning, Adam and Eve
had no sin,

So they had no "sinful nature,"

And yet when presented with temptation,

They took the bait ruining God's perfect creation.

Henceforth, everyone born from them,

Of a different similitude, still sin.

Therefore, those born of the flesh,

Share in the same curse of death.

Yet, God in mercy and grace set about to restore us to
perfection,

Through a substitutionary death and a resurrection,

Which, when believed, gives us a new birth,

Severing us from this fallen earth,

No longer sharing Adam's spiritual nature,

But now brought to life and made a brand new creature,

A miracle solely of God still possessing only one spiritual
nature,

Encased in a body that will also be made perfect at the rapture.

Romans 5:8-15; Romans 6:23;
Ephesians 2:1-9; 2 Corinthians 5:14-21; 1 Peter 1:18-23; Romans 8:9-11;
Romans 8:22-23

DEFACE

If you think that you can add one thing of your own,
To the perfect work Christ did on the cross to bring us home,

You've been deceived and don't appreciate the price,
God the Father paid when His Son He sacrificed!

Thinking you must confess your sins and work your fingers to
the bone,
Shows that you're not resting in Christ's finished work alone!

A perfect analogy for what you do when you mix your own
works and God's grace,
Is to say that you've painted a mustache on The Mona Lisa's
face!

It's just a crying shame and a real disgrace,
To think that you must contribute to what God gave freely as a
gift of grace!

Romans 11:6; Ephesians 2:8-9; Romans 3:21-31
(Acknowledgement to Bob George for the wonderful analogy of painting a
mustache on the Mona Lisa)

PERFECT SACRIFICE

Grace is so wonderful,
Yet many unwittingly spurn
All that grace includes
When they refuse to learn.

They think they know it all,
And must put their two cents in
By adding to the work of Christ,
Obsessively confessing and forever turning from their sins.

They don't understand the New Covenant,
And how by one perfect sacrifice,
God completely took away their sins
Through the only blood that could completely suffice;

Not like that of bulls and goats
That yearly covered over sin,
But by the perfect blood of Christ
That totally and forever removed ALL of them!

Hebrews 10:1-20; Hebrews 9:22-28; John 1:29

LIVE RENEWED

Once you learn to separate in your mind the flesh from your
perfect spirit you will find,
The body follows closely behind.

You will begin act outwardly as you think,
When from fountains of grace you deeply drink.

The focus is taken off of self and behavior,
When depending upon the life within you from the Savior.

Proverbs 4:23; Romans 12:2;
Romans 8:9; 1 Corinthians 2:16;
2 Peter 3:18; Galatians 2:20;
2 Corinthians 5:17

GIFTS

Never concern yourself with what you think you lack,
Because everyone has a gift and that's a Biblical fact!

Since God is the Author and Giver of them all,
In His hand the smallest gift can be greatest of all!

Romans 12:4-8; 1 Corinthians 12:4-18; 1 Corinthians 1:26-28;
Ephesians 4:4-8; Romans 12:1

INTIMACY

God and I alone in a room ....
Because He rose victorious from a tomb,
I can worship Him any place,
And I don't have to go somewhere special to seek His face.

When once the gospel was made simple and clear,
I knew my access to God could be without fear,
Then a Savior, Advocate, Brother and Friend,
Seated me in Heaven and gave me a world without end!

John 4:21-24; Matthew 27:50-51;
Hebrews 4:14-16; Ephesians 2:4-6;
Ephesians 3:20-21

RECONCILED

How could God extend His free salvation and unconditional love,
If He had not already reconciled Himself to us?

All sin was paid for and forgiven at Calvary,
And all that remains for us to do is simply through faith believe.

Believe that Jesus Christ died for all of our sins,
Was buried, and then rose again.

The moment the barrier of unbelief is removed,
You'll be reconciled to God from your side, born again, and made brand new!

Forgiveness is a one-way street paved by God to you,
But total reconciliation requires two.

2 Corinthians 5:17-21; John 16:7-9;
John 1:29; 1 John 2:2; 1 Corinthians 15:1-4; 1 Peter 1:23-25; Hebrews 3:18-19; Hebrews 11:6

A WAY

When you're surrounded and don't know what to do,

Try to remember there's Someone looking out for you,

And the path He once walked was a rough one too!

God is in your future as well as inside of you!

No matter the circumstance He will make a way for the two of you to pass through!

Hebrews 2:9-18; 1 Corinthians 10:13; Psalm 23:1-6; Matthew 28:20; Acts 17:28; Isaiah 43:18-19

ONE/WON AND DONE

In days of old it took sacrifice after sacrifice,
To cover sin and make the people right in God's sight.

The blood of bulls and goats was continually shed,
And the people were ever conscious of their sin, living in a
state of guilt and dread!

It was a heavy load of work and a burden of care,
And the people never really felt that they were quite there!

A gulf lay between them and their God,
Which couldn't be eliminated through animal blood.

Then in the fullness of time,
God sent forth His Son to save the lame and spiritually blind.

He came to earth to be the once and for all time, perfect
sacrifice,
To close the gap and give "whosoever will" eternal life!

With the guilt and shame of sin completely washed away,
Humanity could embark upon a brand new day!

Sin would no longer be an issue between God and man!
Full pardon and total reconciliation was now at hand!

Through the shed blood and sacrifice of Jesus Christ, God's
Son,
For those who believe, salvation is "one/won and done!"

Hebrews Chapter 10; 2 Corinthians 5:17-21; Psalm 118:22-29; John 1:29; 1
John 2:2

JUST ONE LOOK

Just one look at the fiery serpent on the pole,

Saved the people from the bite that could destroy their souls.

Just one look as Jesus hung between heaven and earth,

The condemned man next to Him believed and saw His worth.

Just one look, in faith, when in Jesus our Savior we see,

Salvation becomes ours entirely free!

Just one look...

That's all it took...

Numbers 21:5-9; John 3:13-15;
Luke 23:38-43; John 3:16

UTTERMOST

If you could be good enough to go to heaven,
Jesus would never have come to earth to suffer and die.
The law would have been sufficient for those who kept it,
And would have been able to save you and I.

But the law could only be a mirror,
To reflect our inability and the ugliness of sin.
Those who attempt to keep it,
Walk in the flesh and find they can never rest or win.

That's why God made a better Covenant,
One that is written in Christ's blood.
The Father and the Son made an oath between them,
To save us to the uttermost by Jesus' never ending life and
Calvary's crimson flood.

Hebrews 7:19-25; 1 Peter 1:18-25;
Matthew 26:27-28

IN WEAKNESS

The other day I heard someone say,
"God gives the biggest troubles to those who are strong."
There was a time I might have believed this,
But now I think that is wrong.

We are simply born on a fallen earth
Subject to accident and flawed DNA,
While the world system and the devil himself,
Throw many wrecking balls our way.

But in the midst of the whirlwind I hear God's still, small voice
say,

"I AM with you, I hold you, I care.
I AM forever your faithful friend.
I WILL get you from here to there."

2 Corinthians 12:9-10; 1 Kings 19:11-12; Psalm 46:1-3; Hebrews 13:6; 1 Peter
5:7; 2 Corinthians 1:2-4; Psalm 23:4; Proverbs 18:24;
Matthew 28:20; 2 Corinthians 5:1-8; Psalm 34:17-19

LOVE AND FREE WILL

There can be no love without free will.
It was first in a garden, then from a cross that God made love's appeal.

Now mankind, dead in trespasses and sin,
Blind and apart from God could not win!

For Satan working through the power of sin,
Had us convinced only by our own effort could we return to Him;

But Jesus broke sin's power and hold over us,
When from that cross He cried, "It is finished!"

Of His own good, gracious will,
Jesus still holds out His arms making love's only appeal,

Crying salvation is free to whosoever will,
Come unto me of their own free will!

Answer love's call and the life of Christ will,
In your heart, be completely fulfilled.

Genesis 2:15-17; Genesis 3:4-15;
Ephesians 2:1-6; Colossians 2:9-14; Romans 6:3-14; Romans 8:1-4; Revelation 22:17; John 3:14-21; John 19:30; 1 John 4:9-19

NEVER ALONE

Savior ever with me,
My Lord Jesus Christ!
His grace is sufficient for me
In every circumstance of life.

Were I strong and capable,
Enriched with this world's goods,
I might not lean upon Him,
And trust Him as I should.

So in my humble status,
I can take delight,
For His love and power sustain me,
In my ordinary little life!

2 Corinthians 12:9-10; Hebrews 13:5-6

BEAUTY WINS

There's so much beauty in this world,
And yet with evil it must now coexist.
One lifts us high in spirit,
While the other we must resist!

Though we may struggle upon this earth,
Evil's already a defeated foe.
His head was crushed by Jesus
Many centuries ago.

When Immanuel was born in Bethlehem,
Evil did not know,
That God had an overarching plan,
And to a cross He would willingly go!

There He became the Lamb of God,
The final sacrifice for all mankind's sin,
And upon His death, burial, and resurrection,
Over Satan He did win!

Little did Satan calculate,
When That "corn of wheat" fell into the ground,
All who would believe in Him,
In His resurrection also would be found!

Praise God, that while evil
May bark and nip upon our heels,
Because Jesus Christ is our Savior,
The FATAL wound has already been healed!

Genesis 3:15; James 4:7; John 18:37; John 12:23-25; John 3:16

24

LIFTED

Everyone has their own journey,
a backstory and a load of care,
And Jesus Christ, the Savior, will sweetly meet them there.

He comes not with condemnation,
nor with fire and brimstone from above,
But He meets them on a cross bearing unconditional love.

There He bids them to "believe in me," believe in all that I have done,
And that in my resurrection your salvation I have won!

John 3:14-18; Matthew 11:27-30;
Acts 16:25-32; Acts 11:17; Romans 4:15-25; John 16:7-11;
1 Corinthians 15:1-4

THE MEANING OF CHRISTMAS

God came to earth in a plain lowly birth,
Through the womb of a young virgin.

On a quiet, clear night in Bethlehem,
He appeared on earth as God's love and gift to all men.

The greatest miracle since the dawn of creation,
Jesus came into the world incased in flesh, the incarnation!

He came on a mission crafted before the earth was made.
First in a manger and then on a cross He was laid.

From the moment of birth to the grave,
He did only God's will so that we might be saved!

Luke 2:7-20; John 3:16-19;
John 5:24-30; Hebrews 4:2-3;
Hebrews 9:24-28

DEAR LORD

Help me to appreciate lovely thoughts and simple things,

A snow-blanketed scene and way the red bird sings,

A warm hearth and a cozy home,

A meal in the oven and a room of my own,

A place of sanctuary reserved not only in heaven but one here on earth,

And knowing to You I am of such worth,

Not only did Jesus leave glory to enable my new birth,

But He cares for my needs while I'm camped here on earth.

1 Peter 5:7; Philippians 4:19-20;
1 Timothy 6:6-8; Matthew 6:26;
Luke 12:6-7

BELIEVE

The Lord of Hosts resides within.
He even deigns to call us "friends."

He's not some distant deity,
But Is close as breath to you and me.

He's the reality we live in and I adore.
He gently knocks at each heart's door.

The believer has answered and let Him in.
Won't you do the same, my unbelieving friends?

Believe the gospel with no further delay,
And today will be your "born again" salvation day!

John 15:15-16; Colossians 1:26-27;
Acts 17:24-31; Revelation 3:20;
Hebrews 3:15; 1 Corinthians 15:1-4;
Acts 16:30-31; Luke 19:10;
Acts 4:12; John 3:3-8; John 3:14-18; John 20:26-31

THE GREAT DIVIDE

Humanity is divided into two types,
Those who are in Adam and those who are in Christ.

In Christ, the nature of Adam expressed by sin,
No longer comes from a place deep within.

Believers have a heart from God given new,
The old man crucified with Christ and removed.

The old man born in Adam has been circumcised.
A new spirt and God's nature within us now lies.

One in spirt with God above,
Sin no longer fits the born again child of God like a hand in a glove.

The inner man is now alive and made of finer stuff.
He's no longer of earth so the struggle may become rough.

Suggestions which really come from the power of sin,
Create a conflict inside a mind not completely renewed by Him.

Yet, the victory has already been won,
By the work of and our union with God's only begotten Son.

The Holy Spirit forever sealed within,
Continually opposes the flesh and the power of sin.

The more we realize we've been set free,
From the law, from sin, and who we used to be,

The struggle grows less turning into God's rest,
And we no longer find ourselves walking after the flesh,

But rather expressing the divine life inside,
Because, in fact, the old nature was, in reality, crucified.

Behavior does not mirror the new man overnight,
But it's not who we are nor does it define us in God's sight.

He sees our new identity,
Freed from the earth and the nature of a fallen humanity.

You're not just a "sinner saved by grace!"
You're a Saint of the Most High God and in heaven already placed!

Romans 6:3-6; Ephesians 2:1-6;
Romans 12:2; Colossians 2:10-15;
1 Corinthians 6:17-20; Ezekiel 36:26-27; Galatians 5:16-25;
Galatians 2:20; Acts 15:14

SERVANT, PRIEST, KING

As a suffering servant, at first He came,

A perfect lamb bound for sacrifice.

With shedding of His flawless blood,

He took our sin away in a crimson flood.

Then He resurrected upon the third day,

To place His blood upon heaven's mercy seat.

Now, our Lord intercedes as our High Priest.

He sits glorified at the right hand of God,

Until He returns to earth with a mighty iron rod,

To rule the nations from King David's throne.

Please, God, may the King of Kings and Lord of Lords come soon?

Even so, come, Lord Jesus, God's Servant, Our High Priest and Forever King!

The Lord Jesus Christ, Lamb of God, is ALL those things!

Matthew 20:28; Hebrews 6:20;
Revelation 19:15-16

ONE MOMENT

One moment in time and space,
I'm young again, the pain erased!

It will be better than being twenty-one,
Eternal perfection when my Lord comes.

The thought of this keeps my hopes up high!
I'm so ready to meet with Jesus in the cloudy sky!

This world's not been easy except for a few,
With most of us damaged by its toxic brew.

Thank God I had the Spirit within me as I traveled through,
And the promise of my Jesus that all things will be made new!

Revelation 21:1-6

COMFORT

When my heart hurts or is ill at ease,
God's Holy Spirit comforts me,
Turning my gaze towards eternity.

I cannot despair or be down for long,
For in my spirit rests salvation's song,
Reassuring me that to Jesus I belong.

Then, I free-fall into God's embrace,
 And there's no trial I cannot face,
For my earthly burdens on Him I've placed and the pain is erased!

2 Corinthians 1:3-4; Romans 8:26-27; Romans 8:16-18;
Deuteronomy 33:26-27;
Philippians 4:6-7

MY FATHER IS POWERFUL AND GOOD

My Father's rich and owns the cattle of a thousand hills.
All of my needs on earth He's promised to fill.

He has no hidden agenda or trick up His sleeve.
He never gets angry with me nor is He even peeved.

My enemies may slander, hurl insults, and backbite,
But my Father has told me to leave Him the fight!

For he is ever watchful and He sees my plight,
And He's promised to put all my enemies to flight!

So, I rest knowing Jesus sits in heaven at the Father's right hand.
Our enemies will soon be His footstool and He'll get up and stand!

Then He'll step into the "corridors of light,"
To rescue His bride from earth's coming night!

When He appears in the atmosphere of the first heaven,
That's when I'll FOREVER escape the enemy's malicious, wicked leaven!

In rapture I'll fly with Jesus to the third heaven,
To return to earth with Him after years that number seven.

On white horses we'll come back again,
And I'll watch as He purges this world of all who offend!

He'll set up a Kingdom for a thousand years of righteousness,
And all who enter in will live in peace and be blessed!
Psalm 50:10; Philippians 4:19; Matthew 7:9-11; 1 Peter 5:6-8;

Romans 12:19; Psalm 103:6-14; Acts 9:4-5; Matthew 22:44;
1 Thessalonians 4:13-18; Revelation 19:11-16;
Revelation 20:1-4; 2 Peter 3:13

COMMUNION

Sometimes I look in the mirror into my own eyes,

A window to the soul behind which everything real about me lies.

The outward appearance of the person called me,

Is all that some people know or are able to see.

Ah, but so much resides just past my face,

A world of heavenly thoughts and God's good sweet grace.

Should you peer past my eyes way beyond my soul into that deepest place,

You would see Jesus and me staring back into your face.

As "we" look past your eyes into your soul all the way to your heart,

It's easy to see we are lit within by the same divine spark.

Christ within me and Christ within you,

The Holy Spirit in me recognizes you are a child of God too!

Within this brief communion there is such a sweet pleasure,

Because we know in our hearts we are heirs to the same treasure.

Without even a word spoken we have an unbreakable bond,

Because I'll see you one day in heaven even though on earth we pass on.

Romans 8:16-17; Ephesians 2:19-22; 2 Corinthians 6:14-16

OH, THE BLOOD!

From Eden's sad sunset until time ends,
Salvation is all about "the shedding of blood," my friends...

An innocent lamb sacrificed from the foundation of the world,
While through the pages of history, God's perfect plan
unfurled.

First, through a single man who became a nation,
And a city to give light to the Gentiles, Israel was stationed;

But, sadly, she failed at this divinely appointed task,
And for hundreds of years God spoke His last...

Until bursting forth in the fullness of time,
God, through Israel, became a man bringing light to the blind.

He offered the Kingdom long promised to them,
Yet in their stubbornness and pride, the nation rejected Him.

God knew this would happen all along.
He even had King David speak of it in one of his songs.

The Psalm told how a Savior would suffer and die,
Being rejected, so that He might purchase salvation for you and
I.

All that remains for each person to do,
Is simply believe all the work to save sinners is finished and
through!

Believe Jesus died, was buried, and rose from death just for
you,
And what God said about blood from the beginning is true!

Genesis 3:21-24; Leviticus 17:11;
Hebrews 9:22-28; Revelation 13:8;
Genesis 12:1-2; Isaiah 42:5-7; Isaiah 49:6; Malachi 4:1-6;
Galatians 4:4-5; John 1:1-14;
Romans 15:8; Mark 1:14-15;
Luke 9:18-22; Psalm 22:1,6-18;
1 Corinthians 15:1-4; John 1:29-30

JESUS SAVES

God saw all we would lose from before Eden's garden,
And came to earth in flesh to be our Redeemer bringing us
pardon.

Oh, how marvelous the love of God,
Who showed us our need and then met it in His Son,
Freeing us from the power of the evil one!

He took back earth's title deed,
And made a way back to God for all who will believe.

Believe that he sacrificed Himself for the world's sin, was
buried, and then rose again.

His Spirit will come and live in all who will receive Him,
Living out His supernatural life in and through them.

Oh, the riches of God's goodness and grace,
Which saves those born from Adam's seed, not by their works
but through simple faith!

John 1:14; 1 John 4:2; Revelation 13:8; Galatians 4:4-5; Romans 6:14; 1
Corinthians 15:1-4;
Ephesians 1:9-14; Colossians 1:27;
Ephesians 2:8-9

AUTUMN'S GLORY

Autumn's glory reveals colors of every hue,
When nature falls asleep to spring alive again anew.

Beautiful yet bittersweet musings combine to touch my soul,
As I remember times gone by and the days of old.

'Tis then I seek His comfort and lean hard upon His breast,
As the sweet Holy Spirit beckons me to rest.

Amid all creation's splendor my heart sings in worship to Him,
Because The One who created this glory remains closer than a
friend.

As we face life's winter together in cozy familiarity,
I know the present and the future holds all I'll ever need;

And within this vale of tears He softly speaks to me,
Of an end to seasons of night and a golden bright eternity.

Revelation 21:23; Revelation 22:1-5;1 Corinthians 2:9-10

ODE TO THE WORD AND THE BLOOD

Oh, Word of God,
So powerful and so true!
You're like a brilliant diamond,
With a crimson blaze shining through!

It's the blood of Christ;
The price paid for mankind's sin.
Belief is all it takes,
To catch the fire within.

Hebrews 4:12; 1 Peter 1:18-23;
Ephesians 2:13; Colossians 1:20;
1 John 1:7; Revelation 12:11;
Acts 16:30-31

ENTRUST

God loves your family more than you do.

He created each member as a gift to you.

His heart isn't cold and hard to persuade.

He wanted them saved before you even prayed.

So, just relax, knowing God has a plan.

When you commit your loved ones to Him,

Quietly and patiently entrust them to His loving hand.

2 Peter 3:9; Romans 2:4; Luke 11:11-13;
1 Corinthians 7:13-17; 2 Timothy 1:12;
1 Peter 3:1; 1 Peter 3:7; 1 Peter 3:15-16

HEAVEN'S GATE

I hear them mock and say,
That Jesus Christ is not the only way,
Because all paths lead to God,
And Christianity is just a fraud.

It breaks my heart to hear these lies,
And I want to stand up and cry,
"Don't you know it was the three hours Jesus spent on a cross,
That opened the gates of heaven for all of us?"

What must we do to be permitted in?
Simply believe that Jesus died for our sin,
Was buried and then rose again.
There's no other way to eternally be with Him.

This was God's plan before the world began.
It cannot be topped or altered by man.
By grace through faith in Jesus is the only way.
In this, mankind cannot have his say.

Everyone must bend the knee
And with open hand receive salvation as free.
Best to do so before it's too late,
Because once you die in unbelief you'll never enter heaven's
gate.

John 14:6; Luke 23:44-47;
1 Corinthians 15:1-4; John 3:16;
1 Peter 1:18-21; Revelation 13:7-8;
Ephesians 2:8-9; Romans 1:16-23;
Philippians 2:9-11; John 16:7-11;
Acts 4:12

REJOICE, PRAY, GIVE THANKS

It's easy to grow fearful and depressed,
If we think about limitations more and look to Christ less.

Like Peter who stepped out on a wave,
We have a tendency to look at circumstances and be afraid.

Yet God has told us He'll never leave us to deal with life alone,
And that He would be with us until we reach our heavenly
home.

So, whatever this life throws our way,
We can look to God and happily say...

"Thank You, Lord, for where this will take me!
I'm ever so grateful You will not forsake me!

Help me to do the very best
As I welcome Your guidance through every test.

I know ultimately everything will work together for good
Because in Your Word You said it would!

So, as for me, I'll focus on You and evermore rejoice!
With thanksgiving and praise I'll continually raise my voice!"

1 Thessalonians 5:16-18

IF WE SUFFER

Sometimes when I feel I've been deprived
Of an ease which has blessed others
I remember that life has held far greater strife
For many of my sisters and brothers.

Saints throughout time knew humiliation and loss,
The same as our Lord Who wore a crown of thorns upon His head.
His entire life was lived in the shadow of the cross,
An instrument of death upon which He suffered and bled.

Yet in His suffering for us there is great gain
For it bought us a way back to the Father and eternal life,
Free from sin, death and pain!
Oh, what a glorious future is ours because we are privileged to suffer with Christ!

Romans 8:16-23

THE SECRET TO HAPPINESS

Sometimes I hear a siren call
Tempting me to take a fall
Into a state of discontent
Wondering why and where my blessing went.

But God reminds me from His Word
That I can weld a mighty sword
Against the enemy of my happiness
By simply remembering contentment is the companion of
Godliness.

So rather than being driven by pointless dreams and desire,
Which can rage and burn worse than any fire,
I think of the sweetest One who loves me best,
Who had neither a home or a place of His own to rest.

In gratitude for what I have been given,
Salvation and a place in heaven,
I trust my circumstances here to Him,
Depending on the strength He gives me within.

1 Timothy 6:6-8; Philippians 4:11-13; Matthew 8:20

EVERYTHING IS SACRED

As I walk this vale of tears I never walk alone.
The Savior's always with me,
making my heart heaven's home.

This world's not my friend nor obsession.
Leaving it will be a beautiful release
into the arms of Jesus, my life's only passion.

Yet every little action taken while upon this earth,
Has Jesus at the center and therefore it's of great import.

Whether I'm washing dishes or on my knees praying under heaven's firmament,
Because Jesus and I are united, it's all a sacrament.

.
2 Corinthians 5:5-9; Colossians 3:17; 1 Corinthians 6:19; James 4:4;
Philippians 1:20-21; Hebrews 13:5-6; 1 Corinthians 6:17;
1 Corinthians 3:17b

I REMEMBER

Gazing out a hospital window,
One minute a wife,
The next minute a widow.

Autumn sky and falling leaves,
The Maker of these held me tight,
Just as He cared for the birds in the trees.

The sky didn't change from one minute to the next.
Leaves kept falling as birds continued their ascent.
My Heavenly Father's love flooded my heart continuing to
bless.

Psalm 77:11-14

ABUNDANT

When I was a young Christian I thought
the abundant life" the TV preachers hawked,
Was all about the worldly goods you got.

They implied if you had enough faith in His Word and didn't balk,
Nor engage in any of that devil inspired "negative" talk,

Then God would be pleased and pacified,
Grant your wishes and make you more and more sanctified.

Years of watching how this didn't come true,
Finally made me look at things anew.

Someone was lying and it wasn't me,
Because I knew beyond a doubt that I was saved, you see.

It began to enter into my brain,
That "abundant life" was an entirely other thing.

It wasn't about this world and its goods at all,
But was about how Jesus came to call oppressed people out from under the law.

To call them unto liberty,
To exchange old life for new life, setting them free!

Abundant life means the Good Shepherd knows His own sheep
And is preeminently able to keep,

Them for all of time and eternity,
Guaranteeing their home in heaven and divine paternity.

The abundant life of which Jesus spoke,
Begins with death and for us a new hope,

Not in ourselves or what this world holds, but in our Advocate,
Anchor, and lover of our souls,
The Good Shepherd that bids all to come into the eternal
security of His sheepfold.

John 10:7-11; John 10:27-30;
Luke 4:17-21; John 1:9-17;
2 Corinthians 3:14-18; Galatians 2:16-21; Romans 6:3-18; Matthew 11:27-30;
1 John 5:10-14; 1 John 2:1-2; Hebrews 6:18-20

RIGHTEOUSNESS

One child of God is no more righteous than another,

For we're all given the same new heart that the blood of Christ covers!

Righteousness is Imputed and imparted as a free gift from God,

And there's nothing we do to obtain it that we can brag about or applaud.

All who are born of the Spirit enter a brand new paradigm,

Where they're heaven ready saints in that very moment of time.

If you think you're more righteous than another,

Because your behavior happens to be better than your brother's,

Then you don't understand what it means to be a saint of God,

And you're walking the pathway the Pharisees have trod.

We are who we are by birth and not by our behavior,

Because we've believed the gospel that Jesus is our Savior.

When we believe what God says, that we're saints and not sinners,

The mind is renewed and we live out our identity as mature believers, not beginners.

1 Corinthians 1:30-31; Ezekiel 36:26; Revelation 1:5-6;
Romans 4:20-25; Romans 5:17-19;
Romans 6:17-18; Galatians 2:19-21; Romans 8:9-11;
Colossians 1:27; Colossians 3:3; 1 Corinthians 1:2-3;
John 3:3; 1 Peter 1:18-25;
Romans 12:1-5; Titus 3:4-7;
Ephesians 4:15-24

INFINITE

An inanimate universe without meaning or God,
Is a land of futility, a lonely, frightening place to trod.

Those born in Adam enter the world spiritually dead.
God's all around them but their eyes are blind and their hearts
are like lead.

Yet, with only one glance to Jesus Christ in faith,
The universe becomes a wondrous place where we live with
God forever drinking living water from infinite pools of grace!

Acts 17:24-28; Ephesians 4:17-18;
John 1:9-12; Ezekiel 36:26; Psalm 19:1-3; Ephesians 1:17-23;
John 7:37-39; Revelation 7:16-17;
Ephesians 2:4-8; John 17:20-26

HAPPINESS AND JOY

The Declaration of Independence says everyone has an equal right,

To life, liberty and the pursuit of happiness in this life;

But often the pursuit of these desirable goals,

Leaves us exhausted, disappointed and feeling old.

I have found that happiness is best not pursued,

Chasing after what the world offers that's shiny and new.

A much better path to happiness I have surmised,

Is trusting in the Lord to provide what truly satisfies.

Happiness in this world can be a fleeting thing,

But forever delighting in the Lord gives happiness and joy wings.

Psalm 146:5; 1 Timothy 6:6-8;
Proverbs 3:13; Philippians 4:19-20;
Psalm 37:4-7

THE SEARCH

The conquistadors searched for a fountain of youth,

A poor substitute for the tree in Eden's garden.

Their search proved to be without success or fruit,

Yet blinded mankind still seeks from death an artificial pardon.

Cut off from The Source of life the lost remain,

Parched and devoid of living water,

While feeling their way through the darkness of earth,

Their lives full of vanity and error.

Yet, with God there is a fountain,

Where thirst can be quenched forever.

It is a fountain filled with blood where we find death's true pardon,

And there to His redeeming love the search we do surrender.

Genesis 2:8-9; Genesis 3:24; John 4:10; John 4:14;
John 14:6; Luke 22:19-20; 1 John 5:7-13;
2 Corinthians 5:17-21; John 6:53-58

KING JESUS

There's room enough at the cross for everyone
For God is big and the battle's won.

All humanity, great and small,
Are invited upon Jesus to call.

Every heart's unspoken cry
By Him can be completely satisfied.

Only a Perfect Savior could suffer, bleed and die
For the sins of all mankind.

In Jesus we have a forever Friend
Who stays with us unto the end.

What other King ever wore a crown of thorns,
But the One who rose from death as God's "Firstborn?"

Only a look to Him in faith
Will change a man's eternal fate,

And set him free from the power of sin
The moment the Holy Spirit of God moves in.

John 19:30; John 3:14-18; John 12:46;
Romans 3:22-25; 1 John 2:1-2; 1 John 4:9-10;
John 1:29; Matthew 28:18-20; John 19:1-5;
John 19:17-22; Colossians 1:13-18;
Luke 23:42-43; Romans 6:22-23;
Ephesians 1:13

THE WOMAN IN THE MIRROR

Sometimes I look in the mirror,
And get a little sad at what I see!
The image I behold there,
Isn't the girl who used to be me!

Before I get too discouraged,
The Holy Spirit speaks to me,
Saying that beyond my face and figure,
Is someone of value that He wants me to see!

Then, with a second glance in the mirror,
I can clearly see,
A precious child of God
Is looking back at me!

She's walked through some deep valleys,
And weathered more than a few storms,
But with Jesus as her companion,
She's learned that all is beautiful in His arms.

So, even though on the outside,
The woman in the mirror looks a little worn and her tummy
isn't flat,
She can rejoice in the resurrection and in the amazing fact,
That one fine day her glorified body will rise to a much better
habitat!

2 Corinthians 5:1-4;
Philippians 3:20-21

YOU'RE A SAINT!

Child of God, it takes more faith,

NOT to believe you're "just a sinner saved by grace,"

But rather a totally righteous SAINT!

If a man IS as he thinks,

Then the devil has pulled a massive trick,

If we believe we're still sin sick.

Jesus came to set captives free,

From law, the power of sin and false humility,

So that from a new heart, servants of righteousness we would be!

This is also the gospel, you see....

Romans 6:14,17-18; Romans 6:20-23; Ezekiel 36:26;
2 Corinthians 5:21; 2 Corinthians 5:16-17; Ephesians 2:1-5

THE BOOK OF 1ST IMAGINATIONS

Sometimes I wonder just what book
Most all preachers have mistook,

For the very word of God,
And I find it extremely odd,

That while John the Baptist said
Jesus took the whole world's sin away,
Preachers declare I must confess them everyday,

And that while God Himself calls me a saint,
Preachers say because I still sin, that I ain't!

They further tend to confuse me,
When they declare two people I must be,

Both a saint and a sinner,
And MY hard work determines who's the winner,

And most discouraging of all,
They say that when I sin and fall,

The Holy Spirit's not my rescuer
But plays the role of my accuser!

If that wasn't bad enough,
The thing that I find really rough,

Is when they say God alone does not set me apart,
But I too must play a major part!

Frankly, I see none of this in biblical creed

So I'm thinking the "Book of 1st Imaginations" is what they read!

2 Corinthians 10:5

WOUNDS IN HEAVEN

We all walk a treacherous path on this earth.

Nowadays, evil can even reach us before our birth,

But if we make it safe past that day,

The devil and his minions still toy with us and play,

Their dirty game of destroy, steal and kill,

But that was never God's desire nor His will,

And even though in a fallen world we receive many scars,

Some on the outer hull and some in inward parts,

They only touch the body and affect the soul,

But never reach the perfect spirit where Jesus Christ we hold.

For a very short space of time,

We suffer it seems without reason or rhyme,

But one glorious day we'll escape,

To a totally safe and beautiful place,

Where the only reminder of what we all went through,

In Heaven will be Christ's wounds.

Luke 24:36-47; John 20:24-31; John 14:1-6

BORN AGAIN

First we're born sons and daughters of Adam,

With only the power of sin working through the flesh,

Dead spirits connected to a fallen world;

But with a spark of life from God,

Brought about by faith,

We're taken out of Adam and in Jesus Christ we're placed,

Severed, soul and spirit, from Satan's dark domain,

This is what it means to be born again.

Ephesians 2:1-10; John 3:3-8;
John 10:9-11; John 5:39-40;
John 20:29-31; Colossians 1:12-14;
Colossians 2:10-12; 1 Peter 1:23;
1 John 5:10-13; 2 Corinthians 5:17;
1 Corinthians 15:1-4

SEVEN DROPS OF BLOOD

On an ancient altar, seven drops of blood,
Pointed forward to a crimson flood,
Where on the road to Calvary,
Jesus Christ bled seven ways for you and me.

From the time of Eden's fallen garden,
God decreed only blood could purchase pardon,
And hide from His sight
Sin's unholy blight.

Centuries came and went,
Until the perfect, final sacrifice God sent,
His only begotten Son born sinless of a virgin.
On the cross, the Lamb of God, paid for sin becoming
salvation's Captain.

Because Jesus rose up from the grave after bleeding seven
ways,
We know propitiation has been made,
And by His sacrifice, God is completely satisfied.
Believe this and be justified.

Leviticus 16:14-19; Matthew 1:23;
Hebrews 9:22-28; Hebrews 2:9-18;
Genesis 3:21; Genesis 4:2-7; Luke 22:44;
Matthew 26:67; Isaiah 53:5;
Matthew 27:29-31; Luke 24:39-40;
John 19:34-35; Romans 3:24-26;
1 John 2:2; 1 John 4:10; Hebrews 12:24;
2 Corinthians 5:19-21; Romans 4:25

SHE

She sat alone on the edge of her bed,
Grief and fear gripped her heart.
The prognosis was not good.
She dreaded what she could not stop.

She craved just a shred of hope,
A word of encouragement,
A lifeline thrown to her sinking soul
Drowning in the question of what the future would hold.

She needed God more than she ever had before!
Speaking honestly, urgently to Him,
She said that she would not move from that spot,
Until He spoke to her!

She picked up her Bible, crying what in this situation was God's will,
What in this world was she supposed to do!?
As she turned the page, her eyes fell
On a simple passage that quieted her desperate heart ...

It only took three verses for God to impart to her what was His will ....

"Rejoice evermore."
"Pray without ceasing."
"In everything give thanks: for this is the will of God in Christ Jesus concerning you."

Laying all the grief and fear aside,
For they no longer mattered,
She began to praise and thank
The God who graciously deigned to answer.

1 Thessalonians 5:16-18

THE BREAD AND WINE

The Lord's Supper is not about examining ourselves for how we've performed or sinned.

The Lord's Supper is simply about a celebration of Him!

We remember what He did for us when He went to Calvary,

How much He loves us and how He now lives in you and me!

Just because Paul told the Corinthians to not eat like pigs and get drunk,

That doesn't mean we must be maudlin and in a religious funk.

So friend, if you're a believer in the Lord Jesus Christ,

Rejoice at the Lord's Supper and don't focus on your sins or think about them twice!

In remembrance, happily partake of the bread and wine,

And rest your thoughts upon Jesus Christ, our Savior and the Vine.

Matthew 26:26-28; Luke 22:19-20;
1 Corinthians 11:22-26; John 15:5

THE BIBLE

What if there was as a time machine,
To transport us through history that's not been seen?

Man-made books are full of lies.
We can't know who's really the hero, scoundrel, or spy.

Only one book is totally reliable,
And portrays man truthfully with all his foibles.

This book is a transporter of a kind,
Taking us back to primordial times,

Written by the Spirit of God,
Who brooded over the waters and separated them from dry sod.

God recorded history He saw in His mind before time,
And poetry of His love sublime,

Through prophets, kings and priests,
All penmen in His hand, His amanuensis.

2 Peter 1:21; Jeremiah 20:9;
2 Timothy 3:16; Hebrews 4:2-3

MARRIED TO CHRIST

I'm sure Moses was an exceptional man,

And the Bible says that God spoke to him as to a "friend."

He led the children of Israel from Egypt to the promised land,

And gave to them The Law written by God's very own hand;

But I'll not even "flirt with Moses" while on this side of Calvary I stand,

Because I'm happily wearing my Lord Jesus Christ's wedding band!

Exodus 33:11; Deuteronomy 9:9-11;
Numbers 34:13; Romans 7:1-6;
2 Corinthians 11:2-3; Hebrews 3:1-9; John 1:17

SUIT OF ARMOUR

Every believer has a supernatural suit.
As we stand boldly in it, none can refute,

That victory may always be ours,
For Satan cannot prevail against God's greater power!

His strength in our weakness and the protection we wear,
Covers our backs all the time everywhere.

In the imagination, some like to don the suit each day when they wake,
But, in truth, each piece is already in place.

From the top of our heads to the toes of our feet,
Those who wear the amour of God the devil can never defeat!

Christian, your one offensive weapon is a mighty swift sword,
So learn it and use it, the written Word of the Lord!

In the meantime, just know your helmet can't be removed,
Neither can your belt, your breastplate or your shoes!

With faith in Christ as your shield,
And scripture the sword that you wield,

The principalities and powers of hell
Must flee from before you for against the armor of God they cannot prevail!

Ephesians 6:10-17; Ephesians 3:16-21; Philippians 4:11-13;
2 Corinthians 12:10; Colossians 1:10-14; 1 John 4:4; James 4:7;
Matthew 16:18

CAPTURED BY GRACE

I've been captured
But I don't want to be released,
From the One Who created me
That He might truly set me free.
It's such a sweet state
Standing boldly in grace,
Freed from the shackles of law and manmade religion,
No longer any man's parrot or carrier pigeon.
The thoughts I once lived and believed were so right,
Were really a prison from which I've taken flight.
The chains of false doctrine have fallen away,
And I refuse to revisit them regardless of what others say.

2 Corinthians 3:17; Romans 5:1-2;
Ephesians 3:1-7; Romans 12:2;
John 8:36; Galatians 2:20-21

THE THIEF

I'm so thankful for the thief on the cross.
If not for him many fine lessons might be lost.

Just like with Moses and the brazen serpent on a pole,
The thief could do nothing but look to Jesus to save his soul.

The thief couldn't go anywhere to be baptized,
So all he could do was realize,

That Jesus was Lord, God and King
Able to remember and save him from everything!

One little word of acknowledgment from the condemned man
was all it took,
To save the poor sinner and let him eternally off the hook.

John 3:14-18; Luke 23:33-43;
Numbers 21:5-9

COMPLETELY FORGIVEN, CLEAN AND CLOSE

Years ago all I ever heard from preachers spoken to believers
Was that we were lowly worms,
So before the Lord
We must daily confess our sins and squirm,

Seeking forgiveness incrementally,
So He would turn His face to us again.
He would deign to come close in fellowship
As long as we were ever mindful of, penitent for, and
enumerating all our sins.

That philosophy of man,
Doesn't make much sense in light of plain scripture,
But I was brainwashed by the doctrines of men
And trapped within their religious structure.

But as I rubbed elbows with some graceful children of God,
It began to dawn on me
That not everything I was taught
Was consistent with the fact that in Christ we have been set
free.

The lynchpin of much false doctrine
Comes from an Epistle of the Apostle John.
The single verse of 1 John 1:9
Is where the continual confession of sin comes from.

This verse is much mistook
For many think it addresses believers,
However, it was really meant for The Gnostics,
Heretics who were deceived and deceivers.

They would not acknowledge Jesus came in the flesh,

Nor did they think such a thing as sin existed,
So naturally they did not confess they had ever sinned meaning they did not need a Savior,
Therefore, the gospel they had twisted.

No preacher alive on earth
Can point to a single written verse by any other Apostle
That instructs those who are born again to confess their sins
Because that's simply not New Covenant gospel!

The confession of sin is part of the Law of Moses.
It is Old Covenant and it presupposes
That the final sacrifice has not come,
So the efficacy of Christ's blood, our confession of sin opposes.

The truth is, that the shed blood of Jesus Christ, God's perfect final sacrifice,
Does propitiate and remit all sin.
If believers add their work of confession to the finished work of Christ,
They dishonor Him by saying sin must be paid for and forgiven over and over again.

If we will simply take God at His Word,
Rather than attend to the religious doctrines of men,
We honor the finished work of Christ,
By believing we are completely forgiven, clean and close to Him!

Colossians 2:13; Hebrews 9; Hebrews 10; Psalm 103:12;
Leviticus 26:40-42; Numbers 5:6-7; John 1:29; John 15:3;
Hebrews 13:5-6

A BETTER WAY

Sin, confess, turn
Sin, confess, turn
Sin, confess, turn ...

A never ending cycle by which the religious find pardon,

But God has made a far better way
To deal with our sins by taking them all away!

By one perfect offering of the blood of His Son,
He has perfected forever those who will come,

And rest in the finished work of the cross,
Rather than trying to perfect the flesh by following rules and
keeping laws.

1 Corinthians 15:56; John 19:30;
Hebrews 1:1-3; Hebrews 9:24-28;
Hebrews 10:1-3; Hebrews 10:10;
Hebrews 10:14; Hebrews 10:17;
John 1:29; Romans 6:18; 2 Peter 1:9

RELATE

I don't relate to God
On the basis of the law.

The law was nailed to the cross
And Jesus died after keeping every jot.

The Bible says believers also died with Him;
Therefore, we died to the law and also to the power of sin.

Now because I'm in Him,
Neither the law nor sin can condemn,

And all that's left as a way for me to relate,
Is by God's sweet mercy and amazing grace!

Ephesians 2:8-9; Romans 6:1-18;
Romans 8:1-4; Colossians 2:10-15

BEAUTIFUL STAR

When I was young, I longed for something I did not know,
A craving inside that would not let me go.

I had no idea what it was I might need,
So, inevitably, I looked to the natural world my desire to feed.

I thought from worldly knowledge and education might come satisfaction,
Or perhaps in the stars I could find my attraction,

Or maybe philanthropy might be a good calling,
Something bigger than self that could keep me from falling;

But everything I thought might be the soul's best retreat,
Only made me feel more sadness and empty defeat;

Then not knowing why I did so, I cried out one day,
"God, if you're there either help me or take me away!"

Shortly thereafter the opportunity appeared,
And the gospel of grace I was blessed to hear!

I embraced the truth the moment I understood,
That Jesus was God and the cross was much more than mere wood.

It was an altar upon which God paid for our sins with Christ's perfect blood.
Most importantly, I understood that He rose from the grave and in glorified flesh He once again stood.

Changing my mind about what I believed was true and false,
Made me a new creation and I was no longer lost.

Grace in Rhymes

The Holy Spirit came into my heart,
And sealed me forever so we would never be apart.

All that I once thought might fill me vanished away,
And now the only person or thing I look to is Jesus each day!

He is my satisfaction, my hope and delight,
The Lily of the Valley, the Beautiful Star Who guides me
through earth's darkest nights.

Revelation 22:16; Song of Songs 2:1;
1 Corinthians 15:1-4; 2 Corinthians 5:17-21;
Ephesians 1:13-14

ON WHAT WILL YOU DINE?

Is your comfort zone in Jesus Christ alone?
Or do you prefer the "bread of life" served with a "side" of religion?

Mixing grace and law creates a toxic stew,
That many lap up from their comfortable church pews.

The doctrines of men when taken within,
Are just like the Pharisees' self-righteous leaven.

Mixing grace with some law
Is not God's plan for making us wholly without flaw.

It was six hours on a cross and the glorious resurrection,
That opened to mankind the pearly gates of heaven!

So, please trust in Jesus' sacrifice only,
Because any other scheme means the messenger is accursed and the message phony.

Simply put, Jesus died for our sins was buried and rose again!
On this and this alone I beseech you to depend!

John 6:47-51; Galatians 2:16;
Galatians 2:21; John 6:28-29;
Matthew 16:11-12; Galatians 5:1-9;
.1 Corinthians 1:30-31;
2 Corinthians 5:21; Hebrews 10:14;
Galatians 1:6-9; 1 Corinthians 15:1-4; 2 Corinthians 5:18-20;
Hebrews 2:3

LIVELY HOPE

My hope isn't weak or half dead.
My hope is alive because from God it is fed.

I have faith down deep in my heart
That Jesus, the God man, conquered death's lowest part.

In victory He rose up from the grave,
And His sacrifice means that we can be saved.

The gift of salvation and His life we receive,
When the simple gospel is what we believe,

Trusting He died for all the world's sin,
Was buried and then by God's power from death rose again.

Now, before God we can be justified
As if our conscience or law we had never defied.

On top of this marvelous gift,
We have the assurance that our salvation is kept,

In pristine perfection for us up in heaven,
Where it cannot be touched by the devil's lies or his leaven.

Salvation's a gift that can never be taken away,
Because it is maintained for us by the power of God until the
very last day!

1 Peter 1:3-8; Romans 4:25;
Romans 8:16-17;
1 Thessalonians 5:23-24;1 John 2:1-2;
Romans 3:21-28

GOD LOVES

God loves a bird because it's a bird and loves a tree because it's a tree.
Why wouldn't God love our humanity?

The only thing that ever separated man from Him,
Was the presence of mankind's sin;

But God took care of that situation
When He came in flesh to His own nation,

Ultimately to die upon the tree
That from sin He might set all men free.

Just as the scapegoat took all Israel's sins away,
The sacrifice of Christ did that for the whole world today.

So, all that's left to separate anyone from God,
Is unbelief in His Only Begotten Son!

Just as God loves the birds and the trees,
God has nothing but unconditional love, acceptance and
reconciliation towards all humanity!

God loves!
That's what He does!

Genesis 1:31; Genesis 2:15-17;
Ezekiel 18:4; Romans 3:23-28;
1 John 2:2; 1 John 4:8-10;
2 Corinthians 5:18-21;
Leviticus 16:7-10; John 1:29;
John 1:1-14 Romans 5:6-9;
Hebrews 4:2-3; Hebrews 1:1-3 KJV
Romans 8:1-4

HE TOUCHED THE LEPER

In our broken, fallen humanity,
God doesn't despise us as worthless and unclean.

He simply shows mercy and unconditional love,
And deigns to touch us lifting us up from the mud.

With arms spread wide on Calvary's tree,
He bids us to come to Him and be clean,

Come to the fountain of grace, drink, wash the corruption
away,
Just as He cleansed the leper back in the day.

Mark 1:40-42; Ephesians 2:4-9;
John 15:3; 1 John 1:7;
Hebrews 10:19-22; John 7:37

TAPESTRY

God knows the reason
For each thing that happens in all of life's seasons;

Why sometimes we must hurry up, yet other times we must wait,
And even why we don't make it out of the gate.

We're all engaged in our own temporal race,
Where we face hardships and disappointments and mistakenly call them our fate.

Caught in the middle of life's circumstances sometimes we don't see,
The whole of the forest for all of the trees.

Yet from every single thread of our little lives the Master Weaver is creating a tapestry,
A marvelous display of His grace for all who are watching and the angels to see!

2 Corinthians 4:14-18; Hebrews 12:1-3;
1 Peter 1:10-16; Ephesians 2:6-10;
2 Timothy 4:6-8; Ecclesiastes 3:1-8

I WAS THERE

Over two thousand years ago on a hill called "the place of a skull,"
The One Who made me, the One Who loves my soul,

Stood in the gap for me,
Between heaven and earth hanging on Calvary's tree.

Even though I would not appear on earth for many centuries,
There on the cross Jesus sustained my injuries.

For the punishment that should have been rightfully mine,
Jesus interposed His blood to pay my fine.

So even though my body and soul would not appear on earth until much later,
I was still at the cross with my beautiful Savior;

And wonder of wonders will never cease,
For when I believed the gospel I had the same release,

Off of the cross, buried in a tomb,
Raised from spiritual death to life just as I was also born from a womb.

John 19:17; Luke 23:33;
Galatians 3:13; Isaiah 53:1-12;
Romans 6:23; 1 John 2:2;
1 John 4:9-10; Romans 6:3-6;
Colossians 2:10-12; John 3:3-7;
Galatians 2:20

AT CALVARY

At Calvary God made a better covenant for humanity,

One that could never be undone,

Because it was ratified between the Father and the Son,

Guaranteed to secure for us everlasting life,

Through the power of His endless life,

Supplied to us from up above,

Apart from performance but because of God's mercy, grace and unconditional love.

Hebrews 8:6-13; Hebrews 7:12-16;
Hebrews 6:13,17-20; Hebrews 12:23-24;
Matthew 26:26-28;
John 3:16; Hebrews 13:20

HE'S ALIVE!

I remember
When I realized
Death wasn't the end
Because Jesus was alive!

Before the truth
Was revealed to me,
I felt a sense of sadness over life's futility,
And the coldness of its finality.

I'd been taught that we live and then we die,
And we face nothing but oblivion.
I tried to ignore the specter of death,
But the fear of it stung like a scorpion.

But my soul longed for something more,
What mankind had lost originally,
My heart reached for,
Life lived eternally.

Oh, what joy was finally mine,
When the gospel became clear to my mind,
And fear of death vanished away,
For I knew I'd been saved to a life beyond the grave and time.

Hebrews 2:14-18; Ephesians 3:14-21;
John 3:14-18; 1 Corinthians 15:1-4;
Acts 16:30-34; John 11:23-27;
John 2:18-19; 1 Corinthians 15:55-57

HOW COULD THEY?

How could they not believe
In spite of the miracles they had just seen?

The Only Begotten Son of God cloaked in torn flesh and
humility,
Dying on a cross for the world to see,

Mocked and shamed by hard, cruel men,
And yet while they were doing so He lovingly forgave them.

The light was turned off on the earth
As in privacy Jesus suffered His worst.

Nature even trembled and cried
As the innocent lamb of God was crucified!

In His passion He spoke only seven things,
But with every utterance Jesus fulfilled prophecy and changed
everything!

His words that touch the heart most tenderly,
Were spoken when He cared for His mother so gingerly.

Finally when He paid for the world's sin completely,
He cried out dismissing His Spirit in victory.

Then, something happened that was not forewarned,
As the curtain in the temple from top to bottom was torn,

As God accepted the supreme and final blood sacrifice for sin,
A miracle which opened the gate to heaven so that all men
could freely come back to Him!

Matthew 27:46-54; Mark 15:22-39;
Luke 23:44-47; John 19:26-30;
Philippians 2:5-11

THE WOMEN

Jesus loved women as only God could.
Their hearts and burdens He understood.

They were drawn to the tenderness in Him,
Sensing He valued and genuinely liked them.

He had no hidden or selfish agenda
And they sensed His words were their hope and anchor.

Women loved Jesus during His whole ministry,
Following Him all the way to the cross most faithfully.

When all but John deserted Him and ran away,
The women stayed with Him throughout that torturous day.

So, I find it sweet and consistent with His nature,
That He appeared first to Mary in His glorified stature,

And commissioned her to go to the men and say,
I've seen the Lord and He told me He ascends to our Father
and our God this day!

Matthew 27:54-56; John 19:25-26;
John 20:1-2,11-18

IT REALLY IS FINISHED!

Preachers who teach 1 John 1:9 in error,
Show that they don't understand the covenants God made in
two different eras.

The first covenant He made with Israel and her people as a
nation.
The second He made without mankind's participation.

Now which covenant would you prefer to be under,
One that depends on you to not misstep or blunder?

Or one where the work is already done,
Because the covenant was cut between only the Father and His
perfect Son?

Under the first Covenant you had to continually confess and
sacrifice an animal to pay for your own sin.
Under the New Covenant, Jesus completely paid for and
removed ALL of them.

The truth is that God doesn't remember ANY of your sins,
So why would you need to be continually confessing to obtain
forgiveness and fellowship from Him?

The blood of Christ is simply the ONLY currency that could
forever pay for sin, .
And your daily confessions have no part in erasing them.

Hebrews 8:12-13; Mark 14:22-24;
John 19:30

REMINISCENCES OF A GARDEN

We have a longing for eternity in our hearts,
For we were made in God's image, never meant to die,
And we would have lived forever if not for Satan's lie.

Mankind was given a single law,
Only one choice to make,
Believe the word of God or believe the snake.

They had two trees placed before them in the garden,
One, the tree of the knowledge of good and evil and the other
the tree of life.
The devil deceived Eve but Adam knowingly chose his wife.

When Satan came to tempt Eve,
I wonder if Adam was standing right there,
And why he wouldn't speak up and the Word of God boldly
declare?

One can only imagine how it might have been
Had our original parents made the better choice,
Harkening to God and ignoring Satan's voice!

Thank God that He already had a plan crafted
To restore the erring pair
Saving them from eternal death and separation's deep despair.

As Adam and Eve lived out their time on earth,
I wonder if they reminisced the beauty of their once idyllic life,
When everything was perfection without the ugliness of sin or
strife?

I expect to meet them one day in heaven,

Because God gave them a way back to Him through blood for
sin's remission,
Innocent animal blood until God could come to earth to fully
complete salvation's mission.

Because of the sacrifice of Jesus Christ,
Eternal life can now be everyone's possession
As God restores to those who believe the gospel of grace
Eden's lost perfection.

Genesis 2:7-9,15-23; Genesis 3:1-7;
Genesis 3:8-24; Genesis 4:1-7;
Leviticus 17:11; Hebrews 9:22

NEW HEART/NEW LIFE

At Calvary Jesus took away the whole world's sin,

But a new heart He gives to those who BELIEVE He died for them, was buried, and rose again!

He came that we might have life in Him,

So receive Jesus through faith and be born again.

John 1:29; 1 John 2:2; John 10:9-11; John 3:14-18;
1 Corinthians 15:1-4; Romans 4:25;
Ezekiel 36:26; Luke 22:19-20;
Galatians 2:20; Ephesians 2:8-10;
1 Peter 1:23-25; 1 John 5:11-13

SEATED IN HEAVENLY PLACES

If I'm already seated up in heaven with Christ,

That must mean my spirit's perfectly nice,

With no hint of evil lurking there,

So only one spiritual nature with Christ I share.

No longer is "in Adam" my home address,

But "in Christ" is where I take my rest.

The world may look upon my external self that's passing away,

But God sees my brand new heart and says I'm perfectly OK!

Insulated from all that happens below,

I'm an entirely new creature where judgmental eyes cannot go.

The body will soon die and decay,

But my soul will immediately pass into heaven with my spirit one day!

Ephesians 2:1-10; Ephesians 1:15-23; 2 Corinthians 5:16-17;
Galatians 6:14-15; Galatians 2:20;
Romans Chapter 6; Ezekiel 36:26;
2 Corinthians 4:15-18; John 3:5-8;
1 Peter 1:22-25; 1 John 3:9; Romans 8:28-39;
2 Corinthians 5:6-8

JUST LIVE

It's okay to pace yourself.
Life's a marathon not a sprint,
And it happens in seasons punctuated by seminal events.

Of the works prepared ahead for us,
Often we aren't consciously aware.
We simply walk right into to them not knowing they are there.

It's always in the little things,
And people we least suspect
That God shows forth His glory and through them His will
effects.

Ecclesiastes 3:1; Philippians 2:13;
1 Corinthians 1:25-29;
2 Corinthians 12:9-10

JUST ONE THING

There's only one thing you can do
To cause the Lord to be pleased with you.

That one thing is so easy yet for many it's hard,
Because they like to think they've done their part.

This natural world runs on the basis of quid pro quo,
But in God's economy that just isn't so.

God knows spiritually dead people simply need life,
And trying to perform well only causes them more sin and strife,

Because trying to be righteous in the flesh,
Only leads to pride or discouragement while working hard to do your best.

So a much better way God has made,
For the soul to go to heaven when the body goes into the grave.

He sent His only Begotten Son to earth to live a perfect life under the Law,
So that He could die for the sins of all.

Then the greatest miracle proved Jesus did what He said He would do.
He rose from the dead that He might make a living way to God for me and for you!

The gates of heaven were opened wide,
To all who will receive Jesus' sacrifice,

To all who simply believe He died for their sin,
Was buried and then rose again.

This is the simple gospel and it's all that anyone can do
To please God and receive eternal life too!

Hebrews 11:1-6; Titus 3:4-7; Ephesians 2:8-9; John 5:39-40;
John 20:31; John 10:7-11; 1 Corinthians 15:55-57; Philippians 3:9;
2 Corinthians 5:21; 1 John 5:10-13; Galatians 4:4-7; Isaiah 53:6; Romans 4:25;
1 Peter 3:18; John 2:18-21; Acts 13:28-30;
Mark 15:38; Hebrews 10:19-22;
1 Corinthians 15:1-7; John 6:27-29

ANCHOR

Where is your soul anchored, my friend?

Is it fixed to this fallen world or to a world without end?

Has the old man you were been crucified with Christ?

Have you accepted for yourself His sacrifice?

If not, then will you acknowledge you need Him today,

Believe the gospel, and be saved?

It really is as simple as this:
Jesus died for your sins, was buried and rose from the grave.

The moment you believe this is true the Holy Spirit of God
makes you brand new!

He seals you forever and comes to live within you!

Your new spirit, soul and body all become His,

And with Him here and in heaven you will always live.

Salvation is a gift you can't earn or lose,

Because it's received as a gift from God to "whosoever will"
choose.

Hebrews 6:13-20; Ephesians 2:1-10; 1 Corinthians 15:1-8;
Galatians 2:20; 2 Corinthians 5:17-21; Ephesians 1:13-14;
2 Corinthians 1:20-22; 1 Corinthians 6:17-20;
1 Thessalonians 5:23-24; John 16:7; Hebrews 13:5-6;
John 14:16-18; John 3:16-18;1 John 5:1; Revelation 22:16-17

GIFTED

In Christ we've been taken out of darkness and placed into light.

We've become the glad recipients of grace and eternal life.

No longer are we spiritually connected to this world and the power of sin,

Because we have the Holy Spirit of God within!

The very life of Jesus Christ is ours!

Within our spirit resides a greater power!

No longer must we be the unwitting servants of sin,

Because we have been gifted with wisdom, righteousness, sanctification and redemption!

This is our gifted identity,

And it's real not imaginary!

Colossians 1:12-14; 1 Corinthians 1:30; Romans 6:17-18;
Romans 6:20-23; Ephesians 2:1-10;
Ephesians 1:11-14; 1 John 4:4; 1 Corinthians 6:17;
Galatians 2:20; Colossians 1:27

COMMON GROUND

Apart from Christ, the moralist and the murderer are on the same broad path,

Because in spite of opposite behavior they're both operating in the flesh.

Both are at enmity to God in their own minds,

Even though both had their sins paid for way back in time.

It's simply a matter of faith and how it's been misplaced,

And not having the resurrection life Jesus provided for the entire human race;

But once their minds are turned from unbelief to faith in Christ,

The moralist and the murderer have Him in common and are given a new heart and spiritual life.

Matthew 7:13-14; Romans 8:1-11;
2 Corinthians 5:17-21; Ephesians 2:14-22; Romans 3:21-29;
Philippians 3:7-14; 1 John 5:10-13;
Galatians 6:14-15; Ezekiel 36:26;
Acts 16:27-32; John 11:25-26;
Galatians 2:20

REST

The gospel isn't about what we must do
But rather about what God has done,
And any doctrine that puts the burden on man,
Negates the sacrifice of God's beloved Son.

By grace through faith is the only way
God has given for man,
To die to sin, gain eternal life,
And come back to Him.

Religion is a vain thing,
The devil's trap and invention,
A blight to man causing him unrest,
And filling him with either fear or pretension.

Ephesians 2:8-9; Matthew 11:28-30;
1 Corinthians 15:1-4;
John 3:16; Hebrews 4:10

ANTIDOTE

No matter how dark the night or how deep the hurt,

For the believer's pain there is a powerful antidote.

For every infirmity a "Helper" is there,

Relieving the ache and sharing the care.

Never are we left to cry alone,

For our grieving heart is the Holy Spirit's home.

John 14:16-18; John 16:6-7;
Romans 8:26-27; 1 Corinthians 6:17; 2
Corinthians 1:3-5

PROVISION

The Lord looks after His children in such wonderful ways,

Even when we don't ask Him for things or think to pray.

His blessings rain down from His generous heart,

Also quenching those who from Him are sadly apart;

But the best Gift is lavished on those who are His own,

Because their hearts He has entered and made them His home.

He never tricks us with something cruel or unkind,

But provides all our needs and much more that's so very fine!

Romans 8:26-27; Romans 2:4;
Matthew 5:45; Luke 11:11-13;
Galatians 4:4-7; Philippians 4:18-20;
Philippians 4:6-7;
Ephesians 1:3

THE GOD-MAN

Jesus Christ stepped out of eternity,

"The Only Begotten of the father," that was His paternity;

But our brokenness wasn't His condition,

And He only came to provide for us rendition,

To be the perfect Lamb of God,

The once and forever sacrifice,

Taking away the sin of the world,

The final act of God's plan unfurled.

At the cross of Christ, sin and death were defeated,

And when Jesus rose from the grave Satan's power was depleted.

From death the sting has been removed,

And a better covenant by God approved!

John 1:1-5,14; John 1:10-15;
Hebrews 4:15; 1 John 2:2;
1 John 4:9-10; John 1:29;
Colossians 2:13-15; 1 Corinthians 15:55-57;
Hebrews 8:6-13; Matthew 26:28;
Hebrews 9:14-23

SCAPEGOAT

What did the scapegoat do
With all the people's sins,
Driven out into the wilderness
Never to be seen again?

What did Jesus the Savior do
As He hung on Calvary's tree,
Where He bled and died
For all mankind, even His enemies?

Behold, both the scapegoat and the Lord
Took away sin from among our midst,
With the scapegoat came atonement and with the Lord propitiation,
So that within the camp/our heart God in holiness could exist.......

Now, through faith we receive the Lord's salvation as a completed gift.

1 John 2:1-2; 1 John 4:10;
2 Corinthians 5:18-21;
John 16:7-11; Luke 23:33-34;
Isaiah 53:6; Hebrews 8:12;
Ephesians 2:8-9

RARE JEWEL

There's one thing that brings me to tears,
That stands out as a rare jewel in this world rife with ugliness
and fear.

It's such a simple thing found in subtle little gestures,
Unnoticed by many in a world of narcissistic measure;

A diamond that shines with the most radiant brightness,
To me, is an act of kindness.

Ephesians 4:32; Titus 3:4-7;
1 Corinthians 13:4

WHAT SIN?

Thank God I don't have to recite a litany of my sins,

When I no longer have a consciousness of them.

Your Word says You remember our sins no more,

For they've been removed and You're not keeping score!

At any given moment in time,

There's no mountain of confession I must climb.

There's simply a loving Father, a Great High Priest,

And a throne of grace where I can find rest and sweet relief.

Hebrews 1:1-3; Hebrews 9:22-28; Hebrews 10:1-5;
Hebrews 10:11-22; Hebrews 4:14-16;
John 1:29; 1 John 2:1-2; 1 John 4:9-10;0
John 16:7-11

SAINT YOU

How dare we disagree,

With who God says He's made us to be?

Don't call yourself, "a sinner saved by grace,"

Because if you're in Christ, then you're a bonafide saint!

You ask me how I know this is true .....

My answer is, "Paul called the Corinthians 'saints' too!"

1 Corinthians 1:1-9

TWILIGHT

Somewhere between the day and the night,
I lay me down in soft twilight.

I don't want to break the silence with a spoken prayer,
But within my thoughts I know You're there.

So I blanket myself up in Your love,
Knowing You cherish me from up above,

As loved ones fly across my mind like gentle doves,
I pray they too are carried on the wind of Your sweet love.

Psalm 4:8; John 3:8

VERDICT

My conscience is clean and free

Because of what Jesus did for me;

One sacrifice for sin for all time,

Means there's no mountain of contrition or confession I must climb!

Nothing at all stands between God the Father and me,

Except Jesus, my Advocate and Mediator, Who enters my plea,

And soundly declares me, "not guilty" by reason that He died for me!

On top of this amazing mountain of grace,

God imputes Jesus' righteousness in guilt's place!

1 Timothy 2:5-6; 1 John 2:1-2;
Hebrews 10:1-5; Hebrews 10:14;
Hebrews 10:17-20; Romans 3:23-28;
2 Corinthians 5:19-21;
Romans 8:1-4; John 16:7-11;
2 Corinthians 5:21; 2 Peter 1:2-4; Ezekiel 36:26;
Romans 6:17-18; John 14:6

CHILD

You came to me from God on loan.
You were never mine to keep or own.

I wish I'd known how brief would be the time,
I had to hold your little hand in mine.

I had a few short years to do my best,
Then you went forth to do the rest.

I hope you know of you I am so proud!
In my eyes you stand out from the crowd!

Now, you live so far away,
Where I can't see or touch you every day;

But I'll carry you forever in my heart,
And in the place called "memory" we'll never be far apart.

Psalm 127:3

THE INCARNATION

Jesus left the glory of heaven to be one with us,

Sharing human flesh and blood,

Yet free from the parasite of sin.

Perfection was incarnate in Him!

He was the Grace of God come to earth,

Through the miracle of a virgin birth,

Conceived by the Holy Spirit, Jesus, the only begotten of the Father,

One with Him and yet Another.

How can such a miracle exist?

I don't know but I accept it!

Luke 1:30-35; John 10:27-38;
Hebrews 4:14-15; 1 John 5:5-7;
John 1:1-2; John 1:10-14

PEACE BE STILL

Sometimes, unbidden, memories flood my mind,
Like tsunami waves crashing in from a distant time.

They momentarily overwhelm my heart,
Threatening to tear my peace apart,

Dragging me down into an undertow
Of sad emotions that don't want to let me go;

But then like Peter in the midst of the waves,
I look to Jesus Who always saves,

And speaks peace back to the sea,
Calming the memory of the storms that tried to bury me.

Perched in my "high tower" above the waves,
I look across the seascape that could have been my watery grave,

And thank my God up above
For His salvation and endless love,

Confident there will come a day that memory and tears lie far behind,
Jettisoned into the thing called time,

No longer able to plague my mind,
Wiped from existence by His hand divine.

Hebrews 12:1-2; Philippians 3:13;
Hebrews 6:18-20; Psalm 18:1-6;
Mark 4:39; Matthew 14:22-33; Revelation 21:1-5

HE LEADETH ME

Religion says, "Get busy, there are things you must do!"
Relationship says, "You're my heart, I love you."

Whether sitting at His feet or moving about,
Who we are at the core flows from the inside to the out.

When the flesh rears it's ugly head and we do it's bidding,
The ache in our hearts tells us that we are sinning.

'Tis then the Holy Spirit reminds us of our righteousness,
And guides us down pathways that for us are the best.

Romans 6:6-18; Ezekiel 36:26-27;
Romans 8:9-16; Ephesians 4:30;
John 16:7-11; Hebrews 12:1-11

NEVER ENDING HAPPY ENDING!

The cross is the altar upon which the Lamb of God died,
Laying down His life for you and I.

He had the power to descend from the cross or to stay.
He chose the latter for our sins to pay.

Then He rose from death to give us His life,
Justified before God, delivered from condemnation, mankind's
plight.

While living on earth from salvation to the grave,
We experience tribulation on a road that's tear paved;

But even though on earth we've much pain and suffering,
In Christ, we're all guaranteed a never-ending happy ending!

John 1:29; Matthew 26:50-56;
John 10:14-18; Romans 4:25;
John 16:33; Romans 8:16-23;
John 3:36; Romans 8:1a

SAVIOR

The whole of the Bible from first book to last,

Is all about Jesus Christ and what He brought back;

Eternal life was lost in a garden,

But He bought us all forgiveness and pardon,

And a new life with His Spirit at our core,

Joined to Him forevermore!

1 Corinthians 6:17; 1 Corinthians 6:19-20;
John 10:27-29; John 10:9-11; John 20:29-31;
1 John 5:10-13; Genesis 3:15;
Revelation 1:8; Revelation 5:11-14

LIVE BY FAITH

I don't spend time considering sin!
Why should I when Jesus has purged all of them?

To dwell upon the law, sin and the flesh,
Is no way for the Christian to live happy and blessed.

The justified should live by faith, the law of the Spirit of life and love,
Knowing that the new hearts given them by God fit His Spirit like a glove!

In that holy place no sin can dwell,
Because what God has done, He's done it well!

An un-renewed mind doesn't fully comprehend the new identity,
Nor understand the completed work of Christ that sets the believer totally free!

The good news is that even though it takes a whole lifetime,
God's Spirit constantly works to oppose the flesh by renewing the mind!

Hebrews 1:3; Romans 1:16-17;
Galatians 3:10-13; Romans 6:12-18; Romans 6:12-18;
Galatians 5:1; Romans 8:1-5; Ezekiel 36:26-27;
Colossians 2:10-12; 2 Corinthians 3:17;
1 Corinthians 6:17-20; 1 John 3:9;
Romans 12:2; John 16:13

NO GUILT, NO SHAME, NO FEAR

Dear saint who stumbles, God's not looking to get even with you,
For mistakes you've made nor to make you more true.

He's a compassionate Father who never leaves your side,
Only your imagination and the devil want you, in shame, guilt and fear to hide.

All of the punishment you think you deserve,
Was taken by Jesus when He came to earth to serve.

Now God looks beyond the flesh and your external parts,
Right into the tabernacle of your perfect heart.

He bids you to come boldly to Him with ALL of your need,
Without feeling guilt over what you falsely perceive.

For He is your "Abba" Who tenderly holds you in His hand.
He accepts and lives inside of you regardless of what you have done or where you stand.

James 3:2; Hebrews 10:3-20;
Hebrews 4:15-16; Romans 8:1;
1 John 3:9; 1 Corinthians 6:17;
John 10:28-30; 1 John 4:16-19

LOOKING

I'm looking unto the resurrected Jesus and not my sin,

For every single one of them was buried with Him.

I'll not fall from the grace in which I stand back into the law,

For only by grace have I been made righteous and without flaw.

Just because I can stumble over the flesh,

And behave in ways that don't reflect,

My true nature from God above,

That doesn't mean my identity has not been permanently secured by God in love.

Hebrews 12:1-2; Isaiah 53:6;
John 1:29; Romans 4:22-25;
Romans 5:1-2; Galatians 5:4;
1 Corinthians 1:27-31; Micah 7:18-19; James 3:2;
Galatians 5:16-18; Colossians 2:9-17

ONE THING

There's only one thing you can do

To assure that God is pleased with you!

It's as easy as easy can be ....

In Jesus Christ you simply believe!

Believe that Jesus is God in human flesh,

And that He lived a perfect life so you could be blessed!

He died for your sins to set you free,

And rose from the dead, supernaturally,

So that you could share in His resurrection life eternally!

John 6:28-29; Hebrews 11:6a;
Romans 1:16-17; Galatians 3:8-14;
Acts 16:30-31; Romans 6:4-8;
John 14:9-11; John 3:16; 1 John 5:10-13

ONLY BLOOD

If following rules is how you think you're made right with God,
You've bought the devil's lie and are the victim of fraud!

The only route to eternal life you see,
Is through a blood based economy!

Innocent blood for the guilty must be shed!
This is the only way to bring life to the spiritually dead.

The good news is a one-time sacrifice has already been made,
When Jesus Christ died for mankind's sin and then went into a grave.

Even better news that will transform you and me,
Is that Jesus Christ rose from death to justify and give life to all who will simply believe!

Galatians 2:16-21; Galatians 3:8-13;
Hebrews 9:22-28;
Romans 4:16-25; John 10:7-11

JESUS CRUSHED IT!

Sent to earth on a divine mission planned out in eternity past,
Immanuel, God with us, the long awaited Messiah came at last!

Born sinless of a virgin, a Jew under the law,
Jesus went about teaching and healing those He saw.

His identity was authenticated by the miracles He performed.
All Israel should have welcomed Him with open arms!

Downtrodden sinners flocked to Him like bees in a swarm,
But the self-righteous rulers only offered Him suspicion and
scorn.

Little did they know, when out of jealousy they got Him
sentenced to death,
They were simply fulfilling prophecy by rejecting their God
come to them in the flesh!

When they nailed Him to the cross and callously watched Him
suffer there,
Even Satan had no idea he was really the one being ensnared,

Because, on Jesus, God the Father place all the world's sin,
And even the law against us was nailed there with Him.

In His death, the world's sin was taken away,
And the law was no longer an obstacle with Jesus Christ as the
new Way.

In the resurrection, Satan got the biggest shock,
When with the one-time perfect sacrifice, justification for all
who believe was bought!

Thunderstruck, Satan must have had a fit,
When he realized the work of salvation was complete and for
mankind, JESUS CRUSHED IT!!!

1 Peter 1:18-21; Revelation 13:7-8;
Galatians 4:4-7; John 1:10-18; John 14:9-11;
Hebrews 10:19-20; Matthew 26:52-57;
Colossians 2:9-15; Romans 4:25; 1 Corinthians 2:7-8;
Romans 5:15-21; Genesis 3:15

NOT BY WORKS

"It is finished," words that should bring sweet relief,

Have been ignored or twisted beyond belief!

Those who think they have something to add,

To the work of salvation have been had!

They've listened to religion's hackneyed lie,

That insists some work must also be done by you and I;

Work like "turn from your sins,"

Or "get baptized in water" before you can come in.

They even backload the gospel with "you must also make Jesus your Lord,"

As if they have the power to do that and more,

Than simply look to the Savior in humble belief,

And in that moment of faith find complete salvation and eternal release!

John 19:30; Mark 15:37-38;
Ephesians 2:8-9; Romans 11:6;
Titus 3:4-7; Hebrews 1:1-3;
Acts 16:30-32; Luke 23:41-43;
John 3:14-21; Galatians 2:21;
John 3:35-36; 1 Corinthians 15:1-4

SOAR

Some days I feel like I'm on two tracks!
One takes me higher and the other holds me back.

Earthly matters and transitory things,
Grab my attention and anxiety bring.

The flesh says, "get down in the dirt and even the score,"
But the Spirit says "You're made for the sky so rise above it and soar!"

Galatians 5:16-17; Philippians 4:4-8; 1
Thessalonians 4:16-18

WHAT A BEAUTIFUL POWERFUL NAME!

Father God, in heaven,

Thank You for Your protection!

Your hands unseen hold me safe,

Where no demon can defile our space.

The world, the flesh and the pride of life,

Are the antithesis to my life in Christ.

His name my lips I've trained to speak,

When I am threatened or I feel weak.

To my ears, "Jesus" is a beautiful sound,

For by that name's power the adversary is beaten down!

John 10:27-30; 1 John 2:15-18;
1 Peter 5:6-11; Philippians 2:8-11

IN TIME

Believer, seasons come and seasons go,
But there's one thing I know that I know!

Behind every door and in every storm, Jesus is there to hold
you in His loving arms!

No matter which door you open and walk through,
Your Heavenly Father's already there in time waiting for you!

You couldn't escape Him even if you wanted to,
Because His Spirit also lives forever within you!

Psalm 139:1-12; 1 Corinthians 3:16

TEACHER TEACHER

Sometimes I reflect on my past ignorance,

And feel chagrined at my unquestioning obedience.

I repeated the lies and false doctrines of men,

Thinking I couldn't possibly know more than them.

I'm grateful for a much better Teacher,

Who's infinitely patient and far far greater,

Who waited for the perfect moment in time,

To use the sword of scripture to further enlighten my mind!

John 14:26; John 16:13-15;
1 Corinthians 2:9-12; 1 John 2:27;
Ephesians 6:17; Hebrews 4:12;
Romans 12:2

WINTER

I'm quickly approaching the winter of my life,
Muted now the passion of youth that often generated sadness
and strife.

It's a relief and comfort to be settled in my soul,
There's no need to struggle, prove anything or on to fakery
hold.

All I really need, I have, and God's promises to boot,
Freed from the fear of death and the power of sin with
salvation an absolute!

Now contentment is my desire and also great reward,
For by the grace of God, I survived all that came before.

1 Timothy 6:6-8; Psalm 46:1-5
2 Corinthians 1:20; Romans 6:22-23;
1 Peter 4:1-2 2; Corinthians 7:1;
Philippians 4:19; 1 John 5:11-13

BABY'S FIRST CHRISTMAS

I remember the first Christmas I spent with Christ,
After I learned the meaning of His sacrifice;

How He suffered and died just for ME
As He hung upon Calvary's cruel tree!

Wonder of wonders, He died but didn't stay dead!
He came forth from the grave just like He said!

I knew in a flash that death wasn't the end,
And believing that truth changed my life, dear friends!

So even though I was twenty-eight at the time,
That I first understood the gospel and changed my mind,

I was born again into a new life,
And that very day I became a babe in Christ!

I've matured a lot since that fateful day,
Walking in the Spirit along life's way,

Growing in grace and renewing my mind,
But the wonder of baby's first Christmas is a memory that
continues to shine!

Luke 2:1-16

NEW

Too many believers live with a phantom,
The ghost of who they think they still are,
Fornicator, thief, liar, coward,
They wear these names like a scar.

They don't realize these old behavior labels,
Were put off of them when they were made new,
Born again of the Spirit,
A Saint in Christ renewed!

Buried with Him in baptism,
Raised with Him to new life,
Only one spiritual nature,
Not two people engaged in a perpetual fight.

Now, the world, the flesh and the devil,
Are enemies located without;
But in perfection we're joined to Jesus,
One new man in spirit with Christ in the joust.

Romans 6:1-8; Romans 6:17-18;
Colossians 2:10-15; 1 Corinthians 1:2; Colossians 1:12-14;
Ephesians 2:1-3; Galatians 2:20; Galatians 5:24-26;
Galatians 5:16-17; 2 Corinthians 5:17; Ephesians 4:17-24;
Colossians 3:3-10; 1 Corinthians 6:17; 1 John 3:8-10;
1 Corinthians 6:9-11

PARADISE'S GATE

Of all the things the thief on the cross,
Could have done the fateful day he was saved,
He could only accomplish one of them,
And because of that one thing he's in heaven today!

Did he come down from the cross,
Get baptized and take care of the poor?
Did he confess all of his sins,
And promise every day to make Jesus his Lord?

The short answer to these questions,
Is a simple, "No, he did not,"
But the thief asked a thing of the Lord,
That assured he would never be forgot!

In humble recognition of his own sorry state,
And the goodness and divinity of Christ,
He asked to be remembered by Him,
As he approached death's dark night.

In that moment of dependence and trust,
The thief on the cross changed his fate,
Because with Jesus that very day,
He entered paradise's gate!

Luke 23:33-43; John 3:14-16

TAKE EAT

Like manna from Heaven, God sent His Son,

A source of spiritual life meant for everyone!

All one must do to get their fill,

Is simply believe Jesus did the Father's will,

When He died for the sin of the whole world,

Was buried and then rose from death to purchase the most valuable pearl.

John 6:32-41; John 6:47-51;
Matthew 26:26-29; 1 John 2:2;
Matthew 13:45-46; Ephesians 1:13-14;
Acts 16:30-31; Revelation 22:17

RIGHTEOUS TEMPLE

For many years I listened as preachers told me I was only
righteous by divine decree,
And "righteous" was sort of an imaginary way that God viewed
me.

They said a "sinner" I still must be,
Because two-dogs fought for dominance on the inside of me!

The thing they failed to take into account,
Is that Jesus lives INSIDE of the believer NOT simply without!

The Word says the perfection of God fills my very core,
And that makes me a righteous saint, not a sinner anymore!

So, not only was righteousness something "imputed" to me,
But righteousness was also "imparted" when God made me His
temple and from sin set me free!

Romans 4:23-25; 1 Corinthians 6:19;
Ephesians 2:19-22; 1 Corinthians 6:15-20;
1 John 3:9; 1 Corinthians 1:30; Romans 6:1-7;
Colossians 2:10-13; 2 Corinthians 5:17

BODY GLORIOUS

Perfectly forgiven ...
Spirit perfectly made ...
Soul heaven ready ...
Only the body must be changed.

This perishable clay
Can only live on earth
For it was taken from it
And must be transcended by a new birth.

The dead in Christ await the resurrection,
Where spirit and soul are to the body again wed,
A body made like the risen Christ's,
Now suited to heaven instead.

1 Corinthians 15:35-55; 1 John 3:2;
Philippians 3:20-21; Romans 8:16-18

CONSOLATION

There are times nobody knows,
Of our sadness or how deep it goes;

But there is One Who always stays close by,
To heal our hurts and console us when we cry.

He knows better than anyone
What it feels like to be forsaken and alone.

So when loneliness or isolation presses in,
Simply raise your head and look to Him.

2 Thessalonians 2:16-17;
2 Corinthians 1:3-5; Hebrews 4:14-16;
Hebrews 13:5-6; Psalm 34:18a

THE KEY TO MY HAPPINESS

I like to think of Jesus all the time.
That's how I focus and renew my mind.

When troublesome things come my way,
I go to the Father and I pray,

"Abba, will You take care of this
And keep my heart in perfect bliss?"

Earth's cares and unsubstantiated fears,
Within a day or so disappear.

Sometimes it's even quicker than that,
And trouble is gone before I can say "scat!"

When perfect peace is once again restored,
It simply makes me trust Him more than I did before.

I would that common trials not come my way,
And yet they serve their purpose on any given day.

Because God knows the way that I take,
Relying on Him makes doing life a "piece of cake."

Because none of it is up to me,
As long as Jesus is all I see.

For me, "Looking Unto Jesus" is the key to finding rest,
And to living a life that's happy, golden, and blessed!

Job 23:10; 1 Corinthians 10:13;
Isaiah 26:3-4; Philippians 4:6-8;
Romans 12:2; Hebrews 12:1-3

LIFE CAME DOWN

From eternity past He entered time,
Came as helpless babe one purpose to find.

He grew in stature and in grace,
Here for the salvation of the human race.

For our sins He came to die,
To give eternal life to all who cry,

And find in Him their hope and release,
Salvation to all who the gospel will believe.

Life came down in deepest night,
To deliver men from darkness into light!

John 1:1-5; Luke 2:43-52;
Colossians 1:12-20; John 6:40;
1 John 5:11-13; John 14:6;
John 8:12; John 12:46-50;
Ephesians 4:8-10; Isaiah 9:6

REST

Their preaching left me cold.
They repeated man-made doctrine, oh, so bold;

But who was I to question them,
To do so might be called a sin!

It's a human weakness to desire the herd,
To not make waves or insist another voice should be heard.

Thank God, He finally called me out
Through His Word spoken within not from without;

Called to freedom and separation,
Into a place of relaxation.

Colossians 2:20-23; 2 Corinthians 3:17;
Psalm 23:1-6; Luke 10:41-42;
Hebrews 4:10

UNNATURAL

Because our hearts were made brand new,
Sinning isn't something the born again desire to do.

Any behavior outside of God's will,
Defies our nature and His sorrow we feel.

Though we're already forgiven of it all,
We can still be hurt when we stumble and fall;

But grace abounds to remind us we are loved and who we are,
As the Spirit renews our minds and heals our scars.

Ezekiel 36:26; Ephesians 4:30;
Romans 6:17-18; Romans 5:19-21;
James 3:2; Romans 12:2;
Galatians 2:20; Romans 8:28-34

NO VICTIM CARD

Those who have Jesus Christ in their life,
Are not victims no matter their earthly plight!

Stop calling yourself what you clearly are not,
Remember God's promises and how they were wrought.

No matter what the devil may cook up for you,
Christ meets the challenge to see you through!

Walk in the Spirit, not in the flesh,
On Jesus rely and completely rest.

Acknowledge Him in all you do,
And see how the Lord comes through for you!

Romans 8:31-39; Philippians 4:11-13;
1 Corinthians 10:13; 2 Peter 1:2-9;
2 Corinthians 1:20; Colossians 2:9-15;
Galatians 5:16-18; Romans 8:28-34;
Proverbs 3:5-8; 1 Thessalonians 5:16-18;
Philippians 4:4-7; Hebrews 12:1-4

ONE PERFECT PERFORMANCE

There's no use in looking back,
With either pride or regret.

Only one life can stand the test,
The gaze of God's holiness.

By grace through faith that life has been made ours,
And is now our possession and heart's desire,

One perfect performance and innocent blood,
Washing the memory of sin away in a crimson flood.

Philippians 3:13-14; 1 Corinthians 2:2;
Romans 3:23-28; John 1:29;
Hebrews 4:15; Galatians 2:20;
Hebrews 10:14; 1 John 5:11-12;
Hebrews 8:12

ROADS

When the road is dark and the future doesn't look very bright,
Remember, we walk by faith not by sight!

Think back to what you've already been brought through,
And recall all the things that God did there for you;

How He helped you in the most unexpected ways,
And brought folks around with encouraging words to say!

Remember how He comforted your aching heart,
While you were crying out to Him alone in the dark!

People without discernment or faith might say,
Those things were just coincidences, but God's child knows
they were His lovingkindness on full display!

2 Corinthians 5:1-9; Psalm 77:9-14;
John 14:16-18; Galatians 4:6;
Romans 8:16-18; Psalm 63:3-7

THE LAMB OF GOD

When Jesus suffered upon the cross,

He bore sin's burden for all of us.

Our forgiveness was purchased there.

Only unbelief keeps a man to sin and death ensnared.

Isaiah 53:6; 1 John 2:2; John 1:29;
John 3:16; John 8:36; Romans 6:22-23;
Acts 20:28; John 16:7-11

OPEN ARMS

The greatest need of every soul
Is to be loved and accepted in whole,

Without any strings attached,
A love that will never hold back!

Well, dear friends, that amazing love has appeared,
And you can respond minus guilt or fear!

Jesus Christ, the Holy One, gave His life for you and there's
nothing left to be done!
Now, God can extend unconditional love and life to humanity
through His only begotten Son!

Thank you Jesus for the love that is there for everyone!
Into Your open arms I pray the lost and lonely will run!

John 3:11-19; Titus 2:11; Hebrews 9:24-28;
1 Thessalonians 5:23-24; Ephesians 2:1-10;
Matthew 11:25-30; Romans 5:8;
2 Corinthians 5:18-21

LOVER'S DANCE

It doesn't take much knowledge to enter in.
All that's required is faith in Him.

Salvation is as simple as believing the gospel;
Believing that the substitutionary death, burial and
resurrection makes it possible,

To receive eternal life and live with God,
And to be seated forever with Christ above.

By grace through faith we are saved,
And we should traverse this life the very same way!

Now that's where some folk get way off course,
As they preach and teach for daily life another source.

They say we're saved by grace but kept that way by our own
works,
As they backload the gospel for all it's worth!

Some of us have done this completely unawares,
As we confess our sins and follow man's rules, climbing their
stairs;

When all that we need we already have inside,
Where the life of Christ will always abide!

All we must do is renew the mind and grow in grace,
As we rest in Him and gaze intently at His lovely face.

The Christian life is a lover's dance of grace
And not a competitive race.

2 Peter 3:18; Ephesians 2:8-9; Romans 3:21-25

SHINE

I long for the day I can see,

The creation from corruption set free!

All will be like Eden's garden there,

No sin, disease or heaviness to bear!

Oh, beautiful city up above,

Pray, come to earth shining with the light of God's pure love!

Hebrews 11:8-10; John 14:1-6;
Revelation 3:12; Revelation 21:1-5

EASY RACE

If sin and grace were in a race,
Grace would always take first place,

For at the cross where Jesus died,
Sin was removed and grace multiplied!

So there's nowhere in this world you can run,
To escape the love of God's dear Son.

His arms are always open wide,
So run into them and there abide.

Unbelief is the only hurdle.
God couldn't have made salvation more facile!

Romans 5:17-21; Acts 17:28; John 1:29;
1 Peter 2:24-25; Titus 2:11;
Acts 16:30-31

LET THERE BE LIGHT

I think that two times in my life
God said, "Let there be light!"

Once was before I had a choice,
When my parents and God were love's only voice.

When life was sparked in my mother's womb,
God began knitting me together in that secret room.

He fashioned my physical parts as He foresaw they should be,
And after nine months into the world I was set free.

Body and soul, I lived twenty-eight years on this earth,
With a spirit that desperately needed light and a new birth,

Tied to this world and the powers that be,
In spiritual darkness I couldn't see,

But for the second time in my life God said, "Let there be light,"
And against His Spirit I put up no fight!

The sweet Holy Spirit wooed me and drew me to the light of
Christ,
And the glorious gospel, when believed, imparted His life!

2 Corinthians 4:3-4; Psalm 139:13-16; John 3:5-8;
John 6:44; John 16:7-13; Ephesians 2:1-10;
Galatians 1:15-16; Colossians 1:12-17; Ezekiel 36:26;
Romans 2:29; Galatians 2:20

WHISPERS

When the enemy whispers in your ear,
"You don't measure up and you've much to fear,"

Remember that Christ IS your life,
And He succeeded in doing everything just right!

There's no fear in love!
Regardless of your position on earth, you're still seated up above!

Colossians 3:3-4; Galatians 2:20;
1 John 4:14-19; Ephesians 2:4-10

ALL THINGS

There's something I like to recall,
When I make a wrong turn or when I stumble and fall.

God has made a spectacular promise to me,
One that settles my mind and makes my heart sing!

No matter what happens in my little life,
Even the things that end up causing me trouble and strife,

God will turn to my advantage in the end!
I ask you, "Could one find a better deal or a Friend?"

Romans 8:28

WHAT A FEELING!

What a feeling that causes the spirit to soar,
Those moments when your soul is flooded with peace and joy
from the Lord.

You know down deep in your heart,
All will be well just as it was from the start!

There hasn't been a moment that He wasn't there,
Working everything for good because He deeply cares!

This sense of well-being on outward circumstance doesn't
depend,
But comes from assurance that His Spirt lives within!

Philippians 4:6-7; 1 Peter 5:7;
Romans 8:28; Jude 1:24-25;
Romans 8:31-32; 1 John 5:11-15;
Nehemiah 8:10

REST ASSURED

Life may not be a rose-petal-paved pathway,

But rest assured God's Grace follows us every day!

In Him we live and move and have our very being,

And faith lights our way even if our eyes are not seeing.

The deliverance of the Lord is always right on time,

And situations on this earth can turn quickly on a dime!

So don't be discouraged by a momentary crisis.

Just believe that God is in control even in the midst of it!

Hebrews 11:1-3; Acts 17:28;
2 Corinthians 5:7; Psalm 121:1-8;
Romans 5:1-9

NIGHT TO DAY

A night of evil things
A day of suffering ...

Reaping evil for pure good
Thirty-three years misunderstood ...

Beaten for speaking truth and grace
Rejected and spat upon in the face ...

Reviled by those who should have loved
Descended so far from courts above ...

The cup at last was full
Paid for sin keeping every rule ...

Another night cold in a grave
Then an Angel rolled the stone away ...

Grave clothes left untouched
Not piled together in a bunch ...

His body came back to life
In a flash of blinding light ...

The sacrifice of the perfect Lamb
Accepted by the great I AM ...

The sin debt of mankind fully paid
Believe this truth and be saved ...

Leave the dark and evil night
Be placed in bright eternal light ...

1 Peter 2:6-10; Colossians 1:12-22; 1 Corinthians 15:1-4

SERVANT

What makes a person great?

Is it beauty, wealth or that in the world they carry weight?

None of these things impress our God above,

Who looks for a heart that will receive His love,

Then follow Him to Calvary,

And rise again from chains set free,

Free to minister to others His grace,

To be a servant to our fallen race.

Matthew 18:1-6; Matthew 23:11;
Ephesians 2:8-10; Ephesians 4:29-32

HEAVEN'S DOOR

Nothing causes my heart to sing
Like the hope the resurrection brings!

Eternal life is mine right now,
For in His death, burial and resurrection I am found!

Christ, my life, now and forevermore,
Come, Sweet Lord, escort us all through heaven's door!

1 Peter 1:3-4; Colossians 3:1-4;
Galatians 2:20; 1 Thessalonians 4:16-18;
John 14:1-3

GOLDEN OPPORTUNITY

Most of us in this life,
Have passed on a "golden opportunity," oh so bright!

Whether through ignorance or fear,
Our perception wasn't completely clear.

A chance for earthly happiness or glory may have been missed,
And we look back with regret for not taking it;

But there's nothing quite as sad,
As missing the opportunity in Christ that all people have!

There's only one thing we mustn't let slip away,
For the consequences of that choice last forever and a day!

So if you hear God's voice calling you to believe the gospel of
Christ,
Don't let anything or anyone keep you from receiving God's gift
of eternal life!

Because in the end,
There's only one "golden opportunity" that REALLY matters, my
friend.

1 Corinthians 15:1-4
Hebrews 4

NOT MY CUP OF TEA

The Law of Moses was never my cup of tea,

But preachers kept trying to force it on me.

They sweetened it up with false promises,

That if I tried harder God would be happy with this.

They only focused on the "big ten"

Ignoring that there were over six hundred of them!

Without realizing it they were putting believers under a hex!

I'm so glad I broke free from this!

Romans 6:14; Galatians 5:18;
Galatians 3:1-3; Galatians 3:10-13

TRUTH SET ME FREE

Have you ever felt like Atlas with the world on his shoulders?

You want to be happy but you feel more like a prisoner pounding boulders!

Three erroneous doctrines for many years had me in that state,

Blinded to the second half of the gospel and ALL the glory of God's marvelous grace!

What did I learn that threw the shackles of religion off of me, you ask.

Well, I'll tell you so that in the same freedom you can bask!

Now don't be shocked and don't be grieved,

But 1 John 1:9 is written to sinners, not saints, you see,

And there aren't two dogs fighting inside of you,

Because you have only one spiritual nature, not two;

And as far as being a sanctified saint is concerned,

That isn't progressive and it isn't earned!

All that we are in Christ is perfectly complete,

And we can rest like little lambs at our Shepherd's feet!

Colossians 2:10-12; Galatians 5:1; 2 Corinthians 3:17; 2 Corinthians 5:17;Ephesians 2:1-3; 1 Corinthians 1:2; 1 Corinthians 6:11; 1 Corinthians 1:30-31; Hebrews 4:9-10; Matthew 11:28-30; John 8:32

THE NAME

Whenever I feel alone or I'm afraid,
My prayer becomes just one name,

The name I first called on long ago,
That changed my course and saved my soul!

The only name that comforts me and gives me rest,
Is "Jesus," the name above all the rest!

Philippians 2:9-11; Acts 2:21;
Acts 4:10-12

IN CHRIST

Lord, I thank You for the mercy
You so richly bestowed on me,
And for the abundance of Your grace
That forever set me free!

I never knew how lost I was
Until your Spirit came to me,
And wooed me, oh so tenderly,
To the hill called Calvary.

There I saw a love sublime,
A love I never knew!
My mind was changed instantly,
And I was made brand new!

I've spent a lifetime growing,
In knowledge and in God's good grace,
But my heart's no more perfect this very day,
Than it was when I first believed and looked upon His face!

John 3:5-8; John 12:30-33;
1 Corinthians 1:30-31; 2 Corinthians 5:17;
Colossians 2:10-12; Ezekiel 36:26;
2 Peter 3:18; Romans 5:15-21

About The Author

Kathy is a widow with one daughter who resides in Scotland. She lives a simple life with her elderly parents in Tennessee.

She has spent the past few years sharing the love of Jesus on Facebook and meeting fellow believers in Christ with whom she has formed a "grace family."

Once she learned the fullness of the grace of God and the truths expressed in the New Covenant, without mixture, the poems began virtually writing themselves as scripture memorized throughout the years was filtered in her mind through the prism of God's pure grace.

Writing the rhymes has been her joy and sharing them a delight!

Printed in Great Britain
by Amazon

50206237R00097